Julio Salcedo / Scalar Architecture

Generic Specific Continuum

Generic Specific Continuum Julio Salcedo / Scalar Architecture

Edited by Oscar Riera Ojeda
Foreword by Luis Rojo
Essay by Ivan Rupnik
Text by Julio Salcedo

OSCAR RIERA OJEDA
PUBLISHERS

Contents

> SPECIFIC

"The Dreams of Reason...."
Foreword by Luis Rojo

This book is offered as an introspective reflection in which Julio Salcedo composes an argument able to rationalize and imbue overall coherence to the range of expressions within his work—competition proposals, academic texts, built work, etc. From beginning to end, this transversal, abstract ambition draws a complete professional profile and invites us to re-interpret his work. This would probably be the most accurate summary of this volume.

The book is constructed like a puzzle, with pieces of different kinds and natures interlocking in order to configure a path that completes the argument; a collection of expressions of the same vocation enunciated by various instruments and voices.

The built work of Julio Salcedo has mostly focused on the domestic scale and the interior, but his winning competition entries, proposals and disciplinary writings point in multiple directions and, as he says, encompass all the scales and dimensions.

This is undoubtedly a self-motivated challenge, a commitment to architecture as a disciplinary problem and as a way of thinking. What if the problems of architecture are transversal in nature? If they cover all scales at once? Or, to put it another way: How can the architect ignore the multiple connections that run between objects, cities, landscapes and infrastructure? Even as these artificially constructed connections distort sizes and subvert identities.

The conflation and distortion of the facts and concepts that necessarily connect his transversal disciplinarity illustrate what might seem obvious to many of us: that theory and practice are two interconnected and complementary representations, produced through different media within a single area of expertise: architecture.

The futile differentiation in architecture between conceptualization and production does not lend itself to the simple analogy of the coin and its two sides: there are more than two possible expressions of the same object or purpose. Indeed, the very nature of architecture is a constant back and forth between reality and thought, or between the manipulation of reality and its conceptualization.

On the one hand, we face the inherent complexity of any discipline. On the other, confront the multiplication of imaginative relationships as they exploit the fortuitous and the simulated.

The architect makes few things with his own hands. Therefore it is necessary to emphasize thought and thus knowledge, as the profession's habitual working media. However, the paradox will always remain that architectural thought, its knowledge, is systematically and obsessively focused on the material world of things and objects, on their production and development. And for that reason, the work of the architect is necessarily caught in a circular movement taking it from the ideas to things, and from things to ideas about things.

The recurring arch of this oscillating geometry constitutes an effective analogy of architectural thinking.

Understood as an expression —amongst many others— of cultural production and social activity, architecture combines the aspirations of rationality with the conflations, mistakes and random interference inherent in any real context. On the rational side, by amplifying the patterns that lead to plausible coherent explanations, modalities of thought and control explain architectural facts and procedures. Conversely, the constant interaction with more complex environments inevitably distorts any system of internal laws. This exterior contact increases the complexity of models and opens the way to uncertainty and randomness in production as well as thought.

Therefore, it can be argued that in architecture, message and content do not merely follow linear patterns like vectors or rays. In fact, message and content spread in a pattern more similar to waves, in which the responses are not unequivocal but multiple and distorted, altered by the coincidence and conflations that result in complex statements whose meaning is neither evident nor unique.

It is in this intellectual and generational context that Julio Salcedo's different facets of work—design, intellectual and academic, etc.— voluntarily locate themselves. In this context, architecture maintains a disciplinary autonomy —recognition of its subject's specific knowledge— while its role and profile are diluted as they become immersed in a larger and more complex social, economic and cultural context.

This hybridization of thought, transversal and multidisciplinary, common to all facets of contemporary thought, reinforces the imbrications of architecture with the reality that necessarily inscribes it. And therefore, it enriches the discourse by introducing concepts and ideas that we find not only in the text but in the projects as well.

The first and most obvious concept is that of complexity, whose quality seems inevitably to be contained in a critical discourse that tolerates paradox and encourages hybridization. A concept that extends to both the conceptual and the productive realms, into concepts of intricacy and its non-scalar operations.

The mechanism of continuity —and its opposition to adjacent articulations— necessarily relates to the inclination towards the use of the complexity of approaches or the intricate nature of the schemes.

Continuity may appear on the diagram or in the material, but in both cases it is set to dilute differences in structure, function, material or other factor. Continuity masks one

reality and replaces it with another. It belongs therefore to the order of simulation.

So it is worth asking — what kind of complexity produces continuity? As an operational tool, continuity does not reveal the complexity that lies beneath the appearance of things, in contrast, it builds a duplicate reality characterized by a different figure.

It is not therefore related to the sociological or specific complexity of a given fragment of reality or a particular context. It is, however, the demonstration of a command of the instruments with which the fragment of reality is configured or transformed; the demonstration of the relationship between architecture and perception in the broadest sense of the word.

The dichotomy between the concepts of 'generic' and 'specific' is also a vortex around which many operational decisions revolve. What follows is a commitment to an ambiguous and open thought process, with said dichotomy never abandoning the innate duplicity of the paradox.

In fact, the argument is introduced, focusing on the dual interpretation that generic architecture offers today: on one side it can be understood as that which is typical of the ordinary, as unintended and pervasive but imbued with formal and iconographic values, on the other, the generic can be seen belonging to the open and flexible order of systems and matrices, oblivious to the simplifications of the imposition of a formal, functional, structural or constructive closed model.

It is not, however, a simple desire for functional flexibility. The aim is more ambitious: an architecture capable of interacting with different parameters and audiences without losing control or value. A search involving the replacement of closed objects for open systems that aims to identify and work with mechanisms intrinsically associated with operational complexity, but without renouncing form as the field of activity and expression under the purview of architecture.

The primacy of the diagram in the planimetric configuration is directly related to reflections on the generic and its dual meaning. And so is the metaphorical figure of the "gesture".

Lasso House completely submerges us in this paradox: Are we confronting a diagram of linear continuity or a surrounding gesture? Which operation supersedes the other? Is it the merger of iconographic domestic fragments—porch, entrance, living spaces, etc.? Or is it the unifying construct of a coherent figure?

On the one hand, it is arguable that the diagram leads us to interactive and open configurations, however it also can reduce the problem to a single, continuous, integrated gesture.

Alternatively, the planimetric operations may be interpreted not as a section of an object but as a system of representation and therefore, the expression of a system in dynamic equilibrium operating at multiple levels.

LUIS ROJO DE CASTRO. Architect, professor and theorist, practices in Madrid with Fernandez-Shaw. Their practice builds important public and cultural projects, many of which have arisen from winning competition entries. He graduated from the Escuela Técnica Superior de Arquitectura de Madrid in 1987, were he has been teaching design since 1992 and is currently Associate Professor at the Department of Architecture. Rojo obtained his Masters degree at the Graduate School of Design, Harvard University, in 1989 - the year he received a Fulbright Scholarship, and was Visiting Professor of Architecture at the GSD on a regular basis between 1994 and 1998, and again in 2002. Since 1999 he has been Visiting Professor of History and Architecture Theory at the Escuela de Arquitectura de Navarra. As a result of his academic and research activities, his writings on contemporary architecture have been published in *A+U, El Croquis, Cassabella, Tectónica, Revista Arquitectura, CIRCO*, etc.

Luis Rojo de Castro
Madrid, January 2010

The Generic Specific Continuum

"Architecture is a gesture. Not every purposive movement of the human body is a gesture.
And no more is every building designed for a purpose architecture."
Ludwig Wittgenstein [1]

"Whatever space and time mean, place and occasion mean more. For space in the image of man is place,
and time in the image of man is occasion."
Aldo Van Eyck [2]

This book depicts the process by which two distinct working hypotheses defined two buildings, which in turn generated a discourse. This discourse is the *Generic Specific Continuum*— a transversal ambition that informs, links and enriches our work.

The *Generic Specific Continuum* has a broad engagement and disciplinary focus; it provides an alternative to a flat architecture with too narrow a focus and too simple an understanding of the inter-relations between thought, design and construction.

The terms *Generic* and *Specific*, at opposite ends of the *Continuum*, emerged from the definitions of two of our projects—the SVS House and the Lasso House respectively—as we struggled, and continue to struggle, to produce layered relationships between the available architectural operations—referred to in this text as 'registers'—and their external conditions.

Generic
The notion of *Generic* arose out of the research and production of the SVS House in Maine. Far from understanding the term as anything commonplace or banal, a *Generic* architecture seeks to provide both a reinterpretation of pervasive models as well as engender a semi-abstracted context. It is in this context, when deploying architectural registers such as *configuration*, that the *Generic* promotes a high degree of variable interaction between occupants, components and scale.

Specific
Conversely, the term *Specific* denotes heightened relations between the suitability, perception and context of a given structure. The notion of *Specific* emerged from the research and production of the Lasso House in Spain. Applying registers such as *figuration*, a *Specific* architecture relies on the functional and phenomenal to delineate a structure. In this way, a *Specific* architecture establishes a strong, discreet relation to its context by the augmentation and fabrication of its qualities and predicaments.

The *Generic Specific Continuum* is born from an understanding that between its poles a tension and a productive range exists. In this book, this range is explored in its different facets, starting with a series of texts describing the *Continuum's* dependence on a broad engagement and a disciplinary focus; and ending with four projects that provide a legible oscillation within the *Continuum*.

The following texts also trace the conceptual lineage and cross-pollinations of the *Continuum* in relation to the *larger realms* and define the *Continuum's* disciplinary focus by describing the methods and operations by which we produce our work. In addition, the following set of registers is critical in the way they populate, define and add nuance to the *Continuum: configur-al-ative, loose-ness, open-ended-ness, complexity, intrica-te-cy, adapt-ive, taut-ness, figur-al-ative*. A series of projects of varying scope, scale, and settings, illustrate the operative use and definitions of these terms.

The Larger Realms

Although the broad engagement of the *Generic Specific Continuum* encompasses a myriad of realms —the genetic in life sciences, the interdependence of context in thermodynamics, etc.— it is here distilled into the geographic realm of urbanism and landscape. The *Continuum* oscillates between a complete immersion in the logics of these *larger realms*, and a resistance suffusing architectural scale with them. Our working hypotheses on the Lasso and SVS houses, which became the *Continuum*, started by mining these larger realms of urbanism and landscape for an index of everything *Generic* and *Specific*.

The very existence of the *Generic* and *Specific* hinges on past and present approximations of an understanding of these larger realm paradigms. The observation of different types of urbanities (figurative or configurative, gridded or topographically motivated, etc.), as well as different landscape constructs (productive/agricultural, picturesque, or the newer infrastructural/landscape/urbanisms), have generated a large portion of the understanding of the *Continuum's* production of space, its perception, its expected movements and its programming. In productive cross-pollination, the emergent paradigms in these realms are often intertwined, blurring the distinction between disciplines. The following is an inventory of the larger realm paradigms broken down by urban and landscape lineages as they relate to the *Generic Specific Continuum*.

Urban Generic: In the context of urbanism, in chronological order, the *Generic* borrows from a lineage of flexible urbanisms where overlapped systems engender choice and rich adjacencies. Our first model is the tartan field of functions in the city grid of Miletus. Following this are the mid nineteenth century reinvestments in organization patterns such as Camillo Sitte's systematization and analysis of cities. Much more recently, models akin to Alison Smithson's *How to Recognize and Read Mat-Building* exemplify configurative urban paradigms that reemerged after World War II. This latter model was no doubt influenced by 'systems thinking'—a mode of thinking which understood issues as dependent on their relationships to an all-encompassing system. The impetus behind this post WWII work has reemerged in the work of several new Dutch practices, including the keen observations of Rem Koolhaas. Koolhaas's analysis, in writings such as *Delirious New York*, of the industrial and the Post-Fordist city contributed to the coinage of the term 'generic city'.

Urban Specific: Also through an urban lens, the *Specific* borrows from adaptive urbanizations that favor an intricacy of

 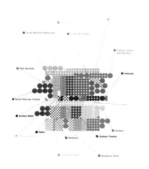  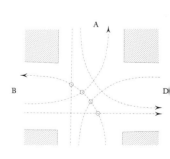

GENERIC <

"There are two kinds of cities,...those based on conscious designs.... and those others that grew naturally, subject to no master scheme but the passage of time, the lay of the land, and the daily life of their occupants."
Spiro Kostof [4]

"...the Picturesque garden is perceived, not as a thing in itself, but as a series of relationships that are gradually revealed to the moving spectator. For Mies, as for the Picturesque landscape designer, the lack of resolution in such contradiction was the starting-point..."
Caroline Constant [5]

activity and movement. The taxonomy of paradigms, in this case, is sparse at best. Hitherto, most of these paths have led to the accretion of either a medieval settlement model, or models where topography dictates morphology. In this vein, the curatorial work of Christopher Alexander and Spiro Kostof has positioned the specific urban paradigm in historical terms only. Likewise, Thom Mayne, of Morphosis Architects, often includes the analogy of a medieval village when describing his own work[6]. Mayne's assembled set of elements conforms to both the idiosyncratic and charged geometries of urban space as well as an amalgam of actions that were meant to take place through a layered idea of time. This referent of the 'medieval village,' in any case, seems both accessible and legible and is a good explanation for a complex assemblage. Our purpose here is to revise the specific so that this referent is not a noumenal construct—the thing itself—but rather part of an operative concept with more registers and depth. As a provisional conjecture, the *Generic Specific Continuum* gives expression to specific urban models as emerging from sedimentation of vectors and the use of adaptive geometries.

Landscape Generic: As with the urban, for landscape there is an equally dense and interlinked range of paradigms that informed the *Continuum*. The generic lineage stems from Ebenezer Howard's notions of programmatic fields in his Garden City proposal. These fields, instead of being designed compositionally, are programmed for different capacities and activities. The generic landscape paradigm culminates in the work of Ian McHarg. Here, the data and constituents of the larger realm become layered factors and aspects of space. Lastly, contemporary paradigms such as Koolhaas's Downsview Park represent an abstraction and extrapolation of Koolhaas's earlier work in the urban realm, focusing, in this case, on the potential of a programmed territory in contrast to his more common referents.

Left to Right :
Miletus by Hippodamus, 53 BC.
Downsview Park, OMA, 2003
Parc de la Villette, Bernard Tschumi, 1982-1998
Camillo Sitte diagrams from *City Planning According to Artistic Principles*
University of Cincinnati Campus Recreation Center Site plan and

Structural plan, Morphosis, 1999-2005
Stourhead Garden, Henry Hoare II, 1741 from Steenbergen in *Architecture and Landscape*
Growth of a Hilltown , from Alexander in *A New Theory for Urban Design*

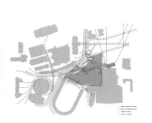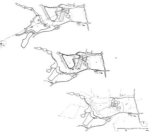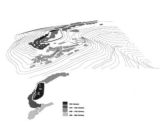

> SPECIFIC

"...mat approach shifts the architect's attention from imagery to organization, and from bounded shape-making to the provisional organization of fields of urban activity, which are understood to have a constant changing character."
Eric Mumford [7]

Landscape Specific: In a way, the *Specific* borrows from what is alluded to in the commonly held notions of landscape—a haptic transverse through a perceptually charged and loose terrain. The *Specific* paradigm in landscape was engendered in the choreography of the Italian Renaissance villa and garden, where the garden became a precise spatial tool in addition to all its intrinsic complexities. The relative ease of manipulation in garden design afforded numerous *Specific* experimentations in the Baroque, but eighteenth century England is where it developed a disciplined instrumentality that sent ripples into the domain of architecture. Gardeners such as Henry Hoare II and Capability Brown redefined the practice from one of landscaping to that of place making. Doing away with traditional and patterned styles, these gardeners invented a syntax of topographic fields accentuated by nodes and field definers in what became the picturesque landscape and complementary notions of the sublime. Examples such as Stourhead defined a spatial realm in which the subject is drawn to an interactive relationship with the elements by means of perception. This instrumentality of perception to choreograph habitation and perambulation later became an operative notion in canonical modern figures such as Mies van der Rohe and Le Corbusier. Projects as diverse as Mies' Barcelona Pavilion and his Friedrichstrasse Skyscraper proposal have as their underlying motivations these series of picturesque landscape methodologies. In addition to the filmic in Le Corbusier's construct of the 'promenade architecturale', the registers of a *Specific* landscape are most effective when objectified in his rooftops or instrumentalized in his definition of 'free' space. Though our own reading of the *Specific* borrows from these modern cross-pollinations, it solicits a higher degree of definition, as well as a tauter relation to phenomena, space and context.

Lastly, the *Generic Specific Continuum* maintains a degree of architectural arbitrariness with respect to its environment. Rather than producing an entropic and flat context, the blurring of boundaries and scales affords a further articulation of space. The study of the 'larger contexts' is not about context in the sense that one examines one's surroundings to produce an appropriately local architecture, fitting for its immediate site. It is about the systemic formation of tools that abstract, stimulate and augment that context. The *Generic Specific Continuum* generates a logic that is related to yet autonomous from an immediate environment. This distancing provokes a conceptual and sensorial awareness. Ultimately, that is the goal of the *Continuum.*

"Today mats are appearing everywhere. We call them fields, grounds, carpets, matrices. The mat answers to the recurring calls for efficiency in land use, indeterminacy in size and shape, flexibility in building use, and mixture in program."
Hashim Sarkis [8]

"The generic urbanism of the urban field does not care for rules.... (it) operates in a free, dynamic network of relations – seemingly arbitrary."
Richard Marshall [9]

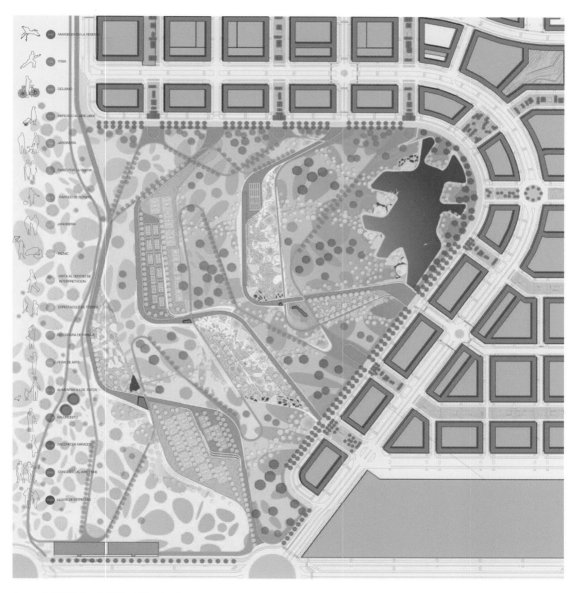

Parque de Valdebebas (with David Fletcher Studio)

"Design is action at a distance. Projection fills the gaps; but to arrange the emanations first from drawings to buildings, then from buildings to the experience of the perceiving and moving subject, in such a way to create these unstable voids....That is where the art lay."
Robin Evans [10]

The Internal Dimensions

If the larger realms provide discernible spatial, phenomenal and programmatic aims, our focus delves equally into the internal dimensions of architecture. These internal dimensions provide an operative context and a set of registers that populate the range of the *Continuum*. A common thread throughout the internal dimensions of the *Continuum* is the reliance on the transformative processes of architectural production and translation. Namely, rather than simply inserting the larger realms into our architecture by scalar shifts, our work co-opts the *larger realms* into architectural registers. In so doing, we prioritize a set of concerns and acknowledge the internal motivations of the work. Effectively, this process is not exclusively architectural, but one of overlays, enrichments and cross-pollination. The working hypotheses of the Lasso House and the SVS house that became the *Continuum* set out to define and curate architectural processes which generate rich and precise *Generic Specific* architectural paradigms. As we developed these two projects a set of internal operations emerged.

The Operative Context of Representation: An understanding of the tools of architectural production, particularly some types of representation, produces incisive and legible translations between ideas, contexts and buildings. The representational range of *Generic Specific* translations provokes a distance and abstraction allowing for an intellectually sharpened intervention in the physical environment. As the Lasso House and the SVS house were developed in different architectural cultures, we are hyper-aware of the role of representation. The notational aspects of representation in Europe are far sparser yet more effective as architects anticipate building through drawing rather than expecting to build through drawing as often occurs in the US. In this light, we see representation as both more limited and more inclusive than its long-held overarching and diluted role in American architecture and theory.[13]

We see representation as more limited because we assume geometry —in particular projective geometry— as the primordial procedure in representation as a means of anticipating the tectonic and physical reality. Projection is the dimension where geometry specifically and representation generally become operative. Rather than limiting the process, the abstraction and precision of projection can provide both clarity and maneuverability. At the generic end of the continuum, and as an example of the operative clarity of projection, the SVS house is an orthographic projective field that captures the

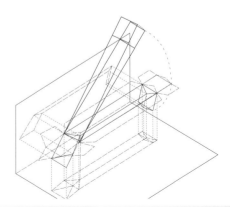

"Investing the maximum potential into the minimum is the aim: if a grid is something ordered and fixed, it is also a map of the random – an ultimate scattering, without bias."
Cecil Balmond [11]

"The logic of repetition, like the logic of statistics..., can be applied regardless of content....What becomes deeply interesting out of this method is pattern...the fundamental quantity of the diagram."
Reiser & Umemoto [12]

algorithmic choreography at its most heightened moment. At the specific end of the continuum, and as example of the unpredictable maneuverability of projection, Lasso House is structured by the hinged projections around the vertical axis. Conversely, we see representation as far more inclusive. Besides postulating a space or a field structure, the precision of representation also:

A. Provides the opportunity to test a limited though heightened phenomenal reality. This is the way the geometry of the entry sequence for the Lasso House is defined.
B. Modulates time and tests the assumptions of accrued uses or users through a structure, creating instantly assumed historical data. In this manner, the constructed topography of the Lasso House is understood as a path both eroded and built up by instant layering.
C. Simulates usage, allowing functions to locate and relocate so as to produce a charged field. As will be demonstrated in later texts, this is the manner in which the arrangement of elements in the SVS house is fixed.
D. Provides the opportunity to examine the metrics of materials and structure as independent and self-supporting arguments.

The deployment of the skin in the Lasso House further articulates the directives of projective geometry by reflecting, continuing, or terminating the skins in their respective locales. Representation beyond this point loses its aura for us; it stops being precise. Tectonic and structural questions are more hands on, more culturally linked and ultimately further engaged in the idiosyncrasies of the project than representation can elaborate. At this point, even though the project remains notational, it shifts to the simulation and management of the built work.

Left to Right
SVS House — parametric field of solids and voids
Recess ceiling panel — geometric formations and forces
Recess communal table – projected geometry

Lasso House – program and form analysis
Lasso House – hinged projections and formation of quadrants
Lasso House – adaptive transformation of wind studies

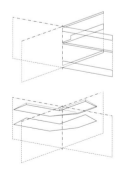

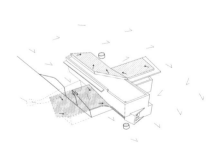

> SPECIFIC

"....each convention of representation implies a convention of perception. Anamorphoses or axonometrics can exemplify this, as they are uncommon in everyday practice, and thus require a conscious adjustment of one's perception. Normally, this need for readjustment occurs in the perception of an outside spectator. But it is especially interesting when the architect shifts perception intentionally within the design process."
Wolfgang Jung [14]

The Operative Context of Internal Dialogue: Our working hypotheses also afforded new understandings *of* the work of several architects in relation to the *Generic Specific Continuum*. As we will see, much of the discussion of the *Generic* emerged from a reading of Alison and Peter Smithson's unrealized project of 1959, in which cleverly augmented modern paradigms create a richly *configurative* and *loose* structure. The positioning of work in terms of the paired registers the *Continuum* generates —such as *figuration / configuration, loose / taut*— is also present in the work of Hans Scharoun. For him, this positioning is both internally and externally motivated. Everyone is familiar with Scharoun's alleged disagreement with Mies van der Rohe regarding the fitness of program to enclosure and whether the enclosure was meant to represent the internal geometries rather than a more legible and abstract volume. Clearly, one could label Sharoun's approach at times as specific and Mies' as generic, yet the breadth of Scharoun's work contains the emergence of configurative practices such as the proposal for Helgoland of 1952. Our work looks at this range within Scharoun's work and others' to help define the operative necessity of a continuum in addressing vastly differing programs and contexts.

Generating the Registers of the Continuum: The internal dimensions of the *Generic-Specific Continuum* are poised to accrue, identify and curate registers, qualifiers and operations that expand their operational capacity. These will be described in further detail, as they tackle, among other issues, program, the temporal aspect of occupation, perception, enclosure, flexibility, and the production of space. The registers expand the *Continuum* from the generic pole to the specific pole and set up sub continuums and pairings that further define architectural operations.
-Registers towards the Generic: *configur-al-itive, loose-ness, open-ended-ness, complex-ity.*
-Registers towards the Specific: *intrica-te-cy, adapt-ive-ed, taut-ness, figure-al-itive*

Left
Helgoland by Hans Scharoun, 1952
Baensch House by Hans Scharoun, 1935

Right
Lasso House

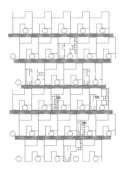

GENERIC <

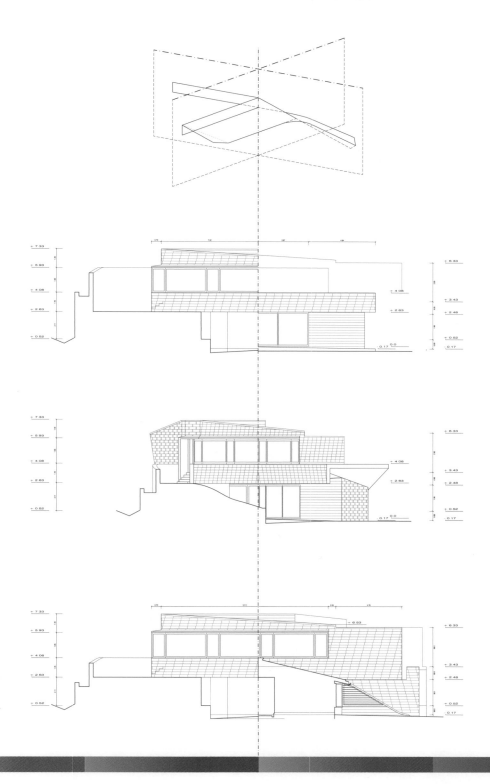

The Registers

CONFIGURAL

LOOSE

OPEN-ENDED

COMPLEXITY

INTRICATE

ADAPTIVE

FIGURAL

TAUT

CONFIGUR-AL-ATIVE

Configuration operates in two main registers. The first one arranges a set of functional units according to their nature, number and characteristics. The second operation hinges on the perceptual complexities arising from the assessment of adjacent but distinct units. This latter operation borrows heavily from psychological studies on perception — termed configural perception. Whether simple or intricate, the units remain legible as sub-elements. In this respect, the importance of each unit is in its inter-relationship with adjacent units, not in its discreet nature. The units are therefore understood in their set rational locales. In other words, it is a syntactical predicament akin to the elements within a language where contextual relationships define roles.

Surprisingly, one of the connotations of configuration is the resultant "shape" or "figure" ensuing from this arrangement. There is consequently, a continuum between figuration and configuration where figurative readings emerge from the configurative field. I do not view configuration as a further substantiation of the double connotation of the term. In chemistry, a configuration is a stable structural makeup of a compound particularly as it addresses spatial relations between atoms. There is a sense, in other words, that this configurative arrangement has locked into a preferred position that gains traction in its use. It generates context in so far as it sets a secondary field within the field of its placement.

> SPECIFIC

1

2

3

4

5

Previous page. Morris Park Supermarket, Bronx, New York 2010
1. Lulu and Mooky's, New York, New York, 2009
2. Lulu and Mooky's, New York, New York, 2009
3. SVS House, Branch Lake, Maine, 2005
4. SVS House, Branch Lake, Maine, 2005
5. Culinary Loft, Brooklyn, New York, 2010

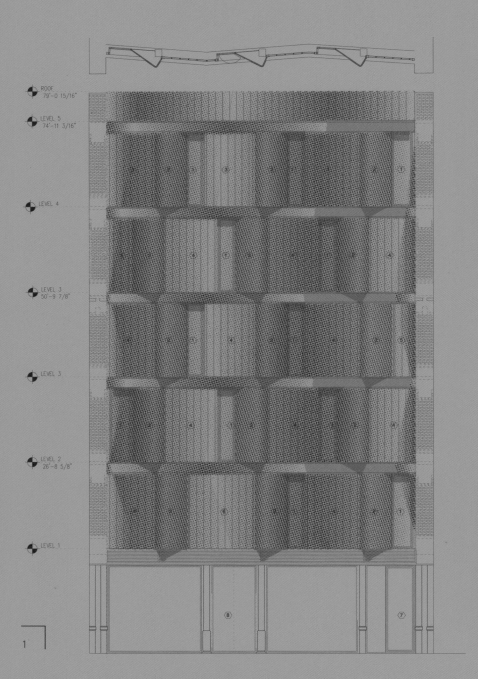

ROOF
79'-0 15/16"

LEVEL 5
74'-11 3/16"

LEVEL 4

LEVEL 3
50'-9 7/8"

LEVEL 3

LEVEL 2
26'-8 5/8"

LEVEL 1

1

2

4

3

5

1. 29th Street Façade Renovation, New York, New York, 2009-present
2. Wellfleet / Woodstock, Wellfleet, Massachusetts, 2009
3. Culinary Loft, Brooklyn, New York, 2010
4. 11 Street Residences, New York, New York, 2007
5. Culinary Loft, Brooklyn, New York, 2010

LOOSE-NESS

Looseness often implies a negatively viewed promiscuity and/or an inadequacy in terms of the relation between parts. Recent studies —like the eponymous *Loose Space*— assert looseness as a productive predicament of space. In the urban realm, loose space is non-programmed and non-hierarchical; it incorporates multiple tasks and is flexible in its uses and habitation. In this respect, *looseness* exists in opposition to institutional space. In the generic continuum, *Loose* is geometric as much as spatial. It incorporates the relationships of spatial boundaries vis-à-vis the interior program. The aforementioned political implications of a resilient occupation and an anti-establishment stance are not of paramount importance, though the question of spatial tolerance is. The essential feature of loose space is a flow of activities from one area to another by means of tolerances amid parts and their boundaries.

Defining Looseness in specific spatial, temporal, or behavioral terms fixes its form...Such is the case with "themed" environments and purified enclaves (Foucault 1997) ...understanding looseness within a dialect where looseness and tightening are in a dynamic relation... Viewing Looseness as a dialectical process reveals its development through tensions: between intended and established activities, rules and meanings and those that are anticipated and might create conflict. Karen A. Franck and Quentin Stevens [13]

LOOSE-NESS

GENERIC <

> SPECIFIC

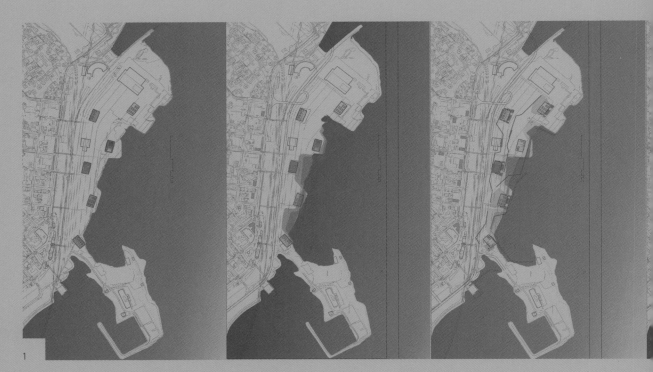

1

3

2

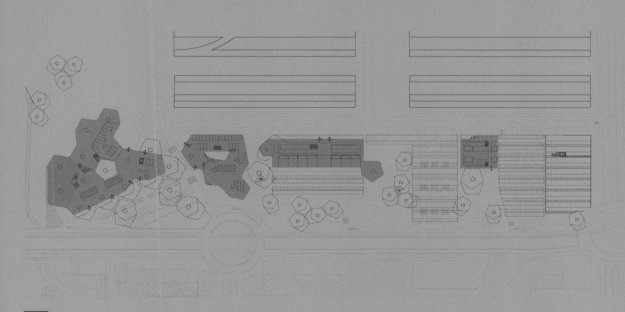

4

Previous page. Los Girasoles Olimpicos, Madrid, Spain, 2008
1. Hamar Development Plan, First Prize International Competition, Hamar, Norway, 2005-present (with Marc Brossa)
2. SVS House, Branch Lake, Maine, 2005
3. Los Girasoles Olimpicos, Madrid, Spain, 2008
4. Los Girasoles Olimpicos, Madrid, Spain, 2008

OPEN-END-ED-NESS

GENERIC <

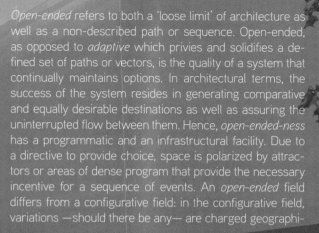

Open-ended refers to both a 'loose limit' of architecture as well as a non-described path or sequence. Open-ended, as opposed to *adaptive* which privies and solidifies a defined set of paths or vectors, is the quality of a system that continually maintains options. In architectural terms, the success of the system resides in generating comparative and equally desirable destinations as well as assuring the uninterrupted flow between them. Hence, *open-ended-ness* has a programmatic and an infrastructural facility. Due to a directive to provide choice, space is polarized by attractors or areas of dense program that provide the necessary incentive for a sequence of events. An *open-ended* field differs from a configurative field: in the configurative field, variations —should there be any— are charged geographi-cally or spatially and not programmatically (e.g. a tenth century mosque in Cordoba.)

In so far as the narrative is not linear but sequential in an aleatory fashion, *open-ended-ness* acts as a complement to the 'promenade architecturale'. However, the result is less a figurative stitching of the structure through a promenade than a complete weave of path across the structure. Julio Cortázar's novel *Hopscotch*, in which, at the end of each chapter, the reader has a choice about what chapter to read next, provides an open-ended counterpart.

> SPECIFIC

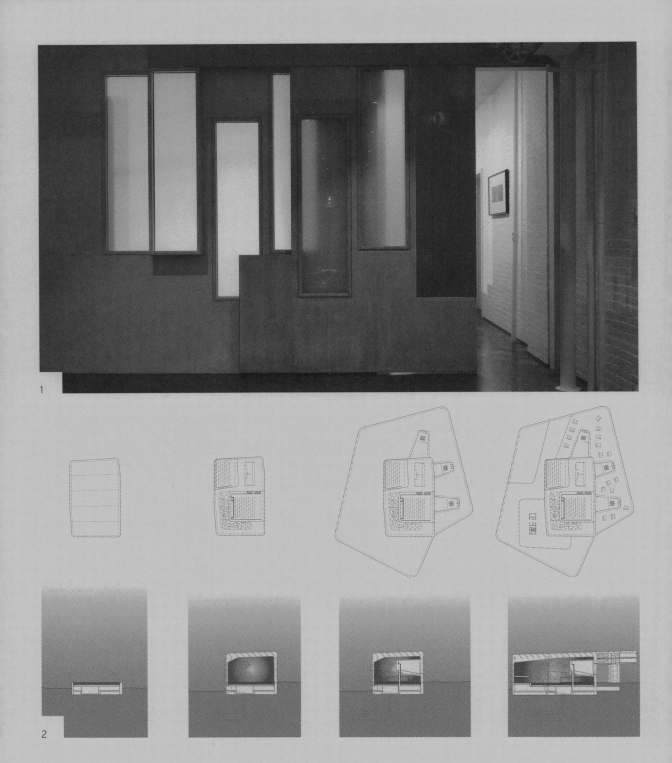

1

2

3

4

Previous page. Hamar Development Plan, First Prize International Competition, Hamar, Norway, 2005-present (with Marc Brossa)
1. Greene Street Loft, New York, New York, 2007
2. Hamar Development Plan, First Prize International Competition, Hamar, Norway, 2005-present (with Marc Brossa)
3. Broome Street Vivarium, New York, New York, 2003 - present (under construction)
4. SVS House, Branch Lake, Maine, 2005

COMPLEX-ITY

GENERIC <

There are events, programs, or positions where the operations of synthesis are either non-operative or non-productive. In these situations, the state of *complexity* affords a directed attitude towards the performance of the numerous elements. *Complexity* curates both the quantity and diversity. The modulation of quantity and diversity gives rise to layered patterns with multivalent readings. The fine-tuning of the conditions of *complexity* comes from the understanding of the ensuing emergent patterns. *Complexity* expresses a condition of numerous elements in a system as well as numerous forms of relationship among the elements.

> SPECIFIC

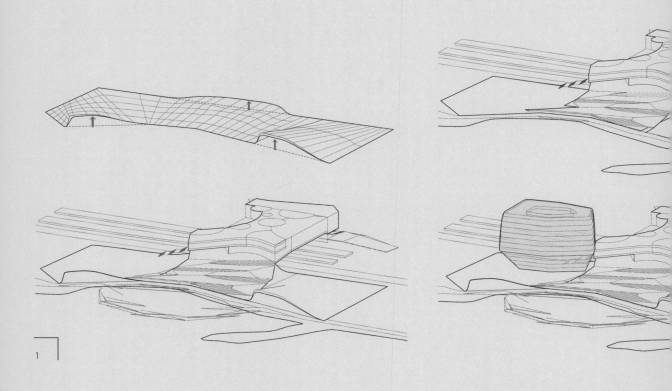

SKYSSTASIONEN STATION RAISED PLAZA CONVENTION CENTER PARKING ESPLANADE LAKE FRO

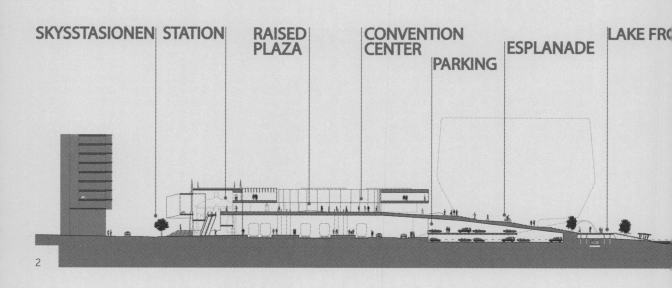

WALK | MJOSA

3

4

Previous page. I + D Housing, Zaragoza, Spain, 2007 (with Marc Brossa)
1. Hamar Development Plan, First Prize International Competition, Hamar, Norway, 2005-present (with Marc Brossa)
2. Hamar Development Plan, First Prize International Competition, Hamar, Norway, 2005-present (with Marc Brossa)
3. I + D Housing, Zaragoza, Spain, 2007 (with Marc Brossa)
4. I + D Housing, Zaragoza, Spain, 2007 (with Marc Brossa)

INTRICA-TE-CY

Intricacy sets the limits of architecture beyond the functional or the responsive and aims towards a protracted definition of architectural structure as a layered, multi-scale formation that has visible traces of its complex design. *Intricacy* demands a raison d'être because, ultimately, *intricacy* highlights the phenomenal and the tectonic. Although *intricacy* does not preclude open-ended social and programmatic architectural demands from materializing, it is not the best venue for their exploration. In our work, *intricacy* affords a more inclusive and exacting relation amongst intended goals: the interaction between habitation, the phenomenal, and tectonic definitions —particularly as they address the *Specific* pole. This protracted investigation of architecture produces a resonance on a variety of different scales, as the issues of habitation and phenomenal/tectonic definitions are amplified and interweaved. Intricacy, like the adaptive, implies a certain sense of duration. It is this duration that both produces the protracted representation of an architectural structure and sees this structure as the registry of a parallel demands.

"Unlike simple hierarchy, subdivision, compartmentalization or modularity, intricacy involves a variation of parts that is not reducible to the structure of the whole.... The term intricacy is intended to move away from this understanding of the architectural detail as an isolated fetishized instance within an otherwise minimal framework. Detail need not be the reduction or concentration of architectural design into a discrete moment. In an intricate network, there are no details per se. Detail is everywhere, ubiquitously distributed and continuously variegated in collaboration with formal and spatial effects. Instead of punctuating volumetric minimalism with discrete details, intricacy implies complexity all over without recourse to compositional contrast. Intricacy occurs where macro and micro scales of components are interwoven and intertwined."
Gregg Lynn

INTRICA-TE-CY

> SPECIFIC

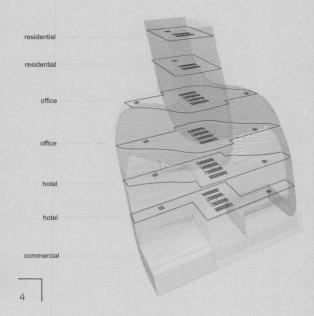

residential

residential

office

office

hotel

hotel

commercial

3

4

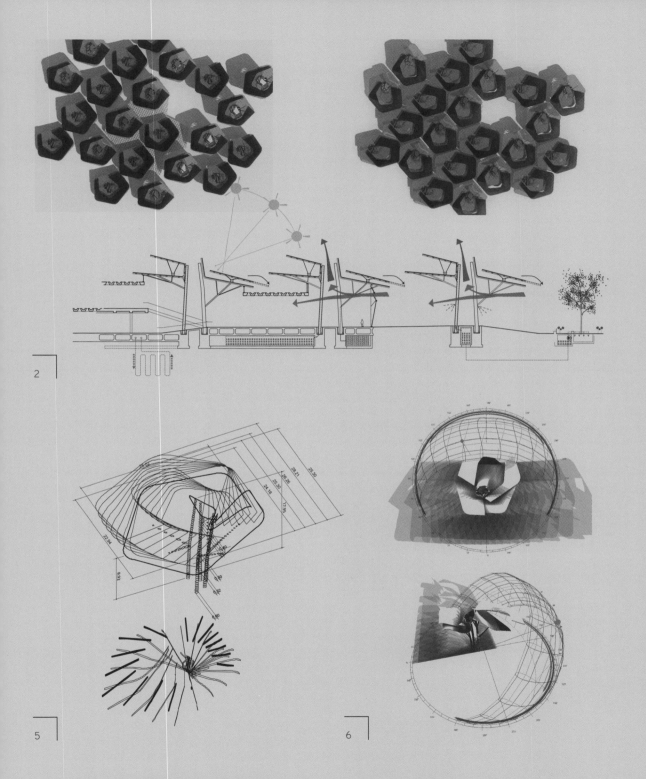

2

5

6

Previous page. Los Girasoles Olimpicos, Madrid, Spain, 2008
1. Lasso House, Trasierra, Spain, 2004
2. Los Girasoles Olimpicos, Madrid, Spain, 2008
3. Hybrid Building Hotel / Office / Apartments, Lahore, Pakistan, 2007

4. Hybrid Building Hotel / Office / Apartments, Lahore, Pakistan, 2007
5. Los Girasoles Olimpicos, Madrid, Spain, 2008
6. Los Girasoles Olimpicos, Madrid, Spain, 2008

ADAPT-IVE-ED

Adaptive sets in motion a process by which a series of actions modify a field structure towards a desired state. In this process of modification a pattern surfaces not as representation of similar gestures, but as the series of traces that accumulate to produce a determined realm/structure. Through the discreet intensification in space, these traces conform to a simulation of compounded intents. This process overall is akin to the sedimentation and erosion of a landscape by active climatic forces or the conforming of an object to the body through use. The chronology of this process is collapsed in the realm of representation. Through representation, architectural design becomes a means to simulate a prolonged process of conformation. The final product remains as a latter instance of the patterns produced by traces.

ADAPT-IVE-ED

> SPECIFIC

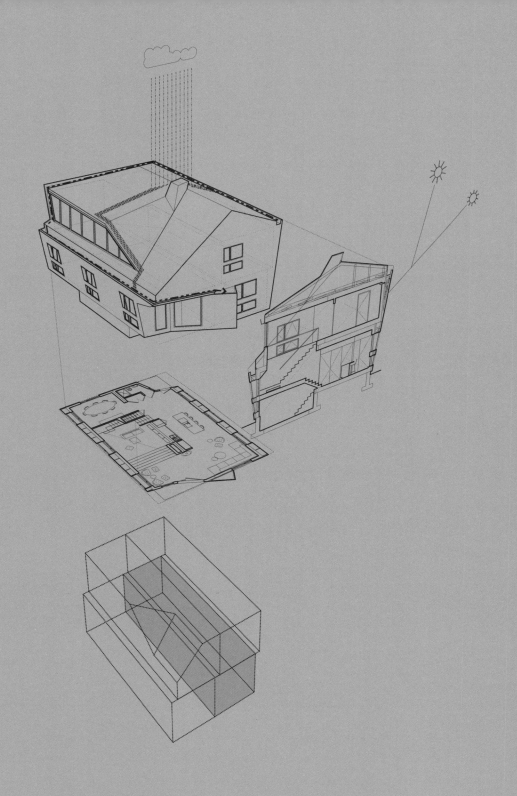

1

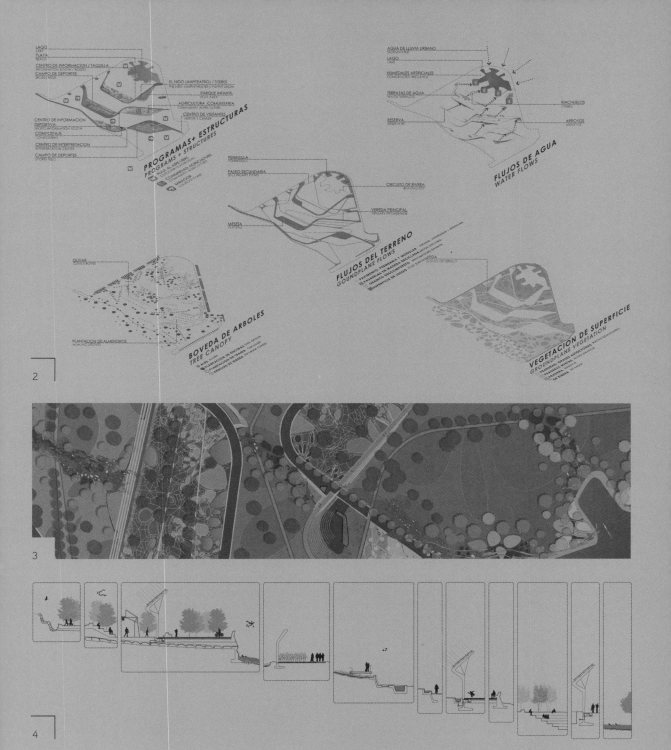

2

3

4

Previous page. "Elements - A Prefabricated Home" Perspective, Sales in the US, 2010
1. "Elements - A Prefabricated Home" Water and Solar Diagrams, Sales in the US, 2010
2. Ambitos Reciprocos, Madrid, Spain, 2009 (with David Fletcher Studio)
3. Ambitos Reciprocos, Madrid, Spain, 2009 (with David Fletcher Studio)
4. Ambitos Reciprocos, Madrid, Spain, 2009 (with David Fletcher Studio)

TAUT-NESS

Taut can be understood in three different ways.

First as the trait of an architecture that is closely draped or structured around a discreet occupation of space. This architectural operation posits the enclosure as a wrapper tightly held around an event that is equally screened and revealed. This event can be a set of idiosyncratic functions in space—in the case of Scharoun's early house designs—or as a spatial structure of heightened phenomenal intensity—as is the case in the passage through the Lasso House as well as in much of Preston Scott Cohen's work.

Conversely, *taut* can be understood as a structure and an envelope that precisely demarcates a legible space. The subject of tightly wrapping in this operation is neither function nor phenomenon, but rather space itself as a legible construct. This sub-category of tautness lends itself to architectures that enunciate Euclidean geometries—such as Mies van der Rohe's Crown Hall. Our project for the Woodstock Museum subjected the building's enclosure and structure to this operation in order to preserve a prismatic extrusion.

Finally, *tautness* elicits a geometric and tectonic condition that is precise in its formation. In topology, the terms *tight* and *taut* describe geometries that are precise and irreducible. A tight curve only has two tangents at any one point. Topologically, the reduction and inevitable performance of these geometries synthesize the architectural efforts of specific architecture. The combination of performative, programmatic and phenomenal objectives is tightly bound into an unequivocal structural arrangement with one singular though complex task.

TAUT-NESS

1

2

4

5

3

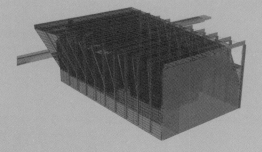

6

Previous page. Wellfleet / Woodstock, Wellfleet, Massachusetts, 2009
1. Syracuse Heart, New York, New York, 2004. See team in credits.
2. Culinary Loft, Brooklyn, New York, 2010
3. Piano Factory Loft, New York, New York, 2001

4. SyracuseHeart, New York, New York, 2004
5. Wellfleet / Woodstock, Wellfleet, Massachusetts, 2009
6. Wellfleet / Woodstock, Wellfleet, Massachusetts, 2009

FIGUR-AL-ATIVE

The *figurative* is an organizational mode that assumes a hierarchy of intentions based upon a string of events. The *figural* requires either the contextual field or a temporal aspect to assertively define itself. In other words, the events in this string are either defined by their relational adjacency to other elements in the field; or the figurative emerges as the sequential accretion of space/time frames. The former is composed while the latter is constructed. Often derided as literal or biomorphic, those assumptions are welcomed into the operation as positive givens. The *figural* in the *Specific* realm is more a directional intention that records itself through time.

In the context of his work on art and craft, Wittgenstein discusses architecture as being gestural. The gesture is a defined event—idiosyncratic in its distinctive proclamation. Though it is not an obvious reading of Wittgenstein, and much less in view of his own house, to conceive of the gestural as a generative force, his observation is welcomed in so far as it bestows the gestural with an attributable rigor and essentiality. Derrida's derision of *figurality* in film as literal is reframed as productive. Literally, the *figurative* is not processed; it is direct. The question at hand is how significant a string of events or adjacencies can be towards the creation of the *figural*.

1

3

Previous page. Lasso House, Trasierra, Spain, 2004
1. Hamar Development Plan, First Prize International Competition, Hamar, Norway, 2005-present (with Marc Brossa)
2. Greenwich Street Loft, New York, New York, 2005
3. Hamar Development Plan, First Prize International Competition, Hamar, Norway, 2005-present (with Marc Brossa)
4. Greenwich Street Loft, New York, New York, 2005
5. Recess, New York, New York, 2009

"Such concerns for individual freedom likewise shaped the Smithsons' designs for urban housing... in "a form of building which allowed them to have the freedom to create a life there... to give them the maximum possibility of choice."

Sarah Goldhagen [17]

The Generic Pole

Our working hypothesis for the SVS house uncovered a series of related principles pointing to the *Generic*. As we developed the house, we uncovered architectural principles of its origins. We layered related issues and delineated a *Generic* pole. A *Generic* architecture promotes by configuration, among other means, a definition of structure and space where parameters can establish the degree of interaction and engagement. The *Generic* is predicated on a parity of spatial elements and it solicits an engagement of choice and relation. The *Generic* registers and modalities are *configural-ative, loose-ness, open-ended-ness* and *complex-ity*.

With regard our discourse on the *Generic*, our foremost intention is to introduce an expanded understanding of the term. Often the generic is understood as the banal and expected mode of production, i.e., off-the-shelf. However, systems of abstract relations also generate rules that are configurative, that evolve, and are suitable for change. The term *Generic* leverages an engendering of quantity with certain variability: a series of elements that escape reification because their arrangement depends on other conditions, oftentimes local, besides "functionality."

As outlined above, a lineage of the *Generic* mode includes Sitte's systemic urban studies, the programmed landscapes of Ebenezer Howard's Garden City, the adaptability and inter-relationship of programs and functions in the 'mat building' movement, and Koolhaas's *Delirious New York*. Recently, the *Generic*, in practices such as MVRDV, has been twofold. On the one hand, it relies on abstract systems. "The design itself is an 'abstract system', a machine that, within the margins dictated by third parties, generates as many differences as possible in order to accommodate as many individuals as possible".[21] On the other hand, the work is clearly more operative in assembling borrowed typologies. Such is the case with MVRDV's Expo 2000 NL Pavilion in Hanover, Germany; it realigns banal phenomena.

Our interest in the generic arose out of a heavy and aleatory demand on architecture. We work to ameliorate the disparate peripheral conditions of Madrid, where utopias like Arturo Soria y Mata's 'Cuidad Lineal' ('Linear City') share space with spontaneous growth models and postmodern urbanisms. In our Madrid work, our architecture is made to be adaptable, to incorporate different programs and morphologies and to establish inter-relationships and programmed spaces where there are none. Our studies show that Linear City has indeed managed to provide a program density and variety, but that there is also a necessity to engender forms out of those relations; forms that would mediate the peripheral extremes. This expanded framing of the term *Generic* defines a mode for architecture to engage various complex phenomena at the urban and territorial scales.

"The Generic City is sociology happening."
Rem Koolhaas [18]

"The generic is the lowest form register of singularity amongst a broad sample of cases."
FOA [19]

"The term generic, as I use it, refers to the not-yet-designed rather than the ordinary or everyday, the average....
More in the spirit of life sciences it is the yet-to-be-specified."
Gregg Lynn [20]

After our first work in Madrid, we went back to the sources of 'systems thinking'—frameworks that understand problems as part of larger systems—and its application to architecture. This search yielded a new understanding of architecture that was previously only conceived as late modern—most notably in the work of Peter and Alison Smithson. Even before Alison Smithson's essay *How to Recognize and Read Mat-Building* from 1974, their work had been grappling with the consequences of the *Generic*. Alison and Peter Smithson's Retirement Home project of 1959 departs from the modern canon and points to other concerns such as the complexities of habitation presented by programmatic overlaps. In this project, there are borrowed typologies and elements. At first glance, the project appears as a quotidian Mies plan, but upon further examination, the elements and their inter-relations exceed a Miesian composition. A paradigm shift occurs and another definition of the generic emerges as a complex configurative system.

In the Smithsons' departure from modernism, an emphasis in the variation and reiteration of form and program was imbued with political and philosophical considerations: "Such concerns for individual freedom likewise shaped the Smithsons' designs for urban housing... in a form of building which allowed them to have the freedom to create a life there... to give them the maximum possibility of choice."[22] The contem-

porary notions of the Generic continue to be imbued with socio-psychological considerations. Rather than highlighting the aesthetic or phenomenal, other's concerns with the *Generic* only involve human interaction. In this respect, this discourse remains very much one of 'architecture as a last resort'. In Koolhaas's own terms in *S, M, L, XL* "The Generic city is sociology happening."[23] This point of view is an amelioratory nihilist rendition of modernism: architecture as a mere distributor of social functions.

Surprisingly, in our work the byproduct of a generic architecture can be an equally compelling phenomenal and aesthetic environment. Moreover, we uncovered more facets to the *Generic* in which it can be construed as a productive and nuanced territory for architecture and its context. The SVS house and other following works provide a window into a rich context of *Generic* architectural types as well as a series of registers that expand the programmatic, formal and spatial nature of the *Generic*.

Left to Right :
Retirement Home project , Alison and Peter Smithson, 1959
Silodam, MVRDV, 1995-2003

Yokohama, OMA, 1992
Expo 2000 NL Pavilion, MVRDV, 1997-2000
Les Halles, OMA, 2003

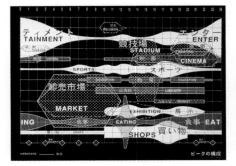

The Specific Pole

Our working hypothesis for the Lasso House revealed a set of preoccupations leading to the *Specific*. As we developed the house, we found we lacked the complementary terms to elaborate the project. We incorporated related contextual and formal issues into our discussion and delineated a *Specific* pole.

A specific architecture accentuates by figuration the suitability of a structure and a space. The specific amplifies a set of functional and phenomenal responses to invariably define and differentiate a structure and a space so that discrete relations can take place between its occupation and context. The *Specific* registers and modalities are *intrica-te-cy*, *adapt-ive-ed*, *taut-ness*, and *figure-al-ative*.

There are two salient facets to the specific: a phenomenal coupling between subject and surroundings, and a complementary notion of a layered space and time. Regarding the coupling of the subject and surroundings, at the time when I attended school, postmodern subjectivity reintroduced a sense of spatial phenomenal awareness that had not been foregrounded by the precepts of conventional modernism. It is not that phenomenal elements were not present in architecture, but that they were not construed as operative and self-sufficient. The rise of representation, and more specifically perspective, was a result of this rise of the phenomenal. Representation and perspective were explorations into a more exacting coupling of the subject and its surroundings. Rather than the political ramifications of a subjective critique

of the modern, it is this operative facet of architecture that the specific is concerned with — the efficacy of the coupling between a legible experience and a structure.

The current work on representation and perspective can be traced to the Renaissance. In Piero della Francesca's "Rotated Orthographic Projection"—shown in Robin Evans's *The Projective Cast*—there is an instance of two-point perspective in which a conic projection more closely anticipates the human gaze. The drawing elucidates, in this manner, the possible relations between geometry and perception. More recently, Preston Scott Cohen has unearthed this body of work and its continued application in other fields such as engineering. Cohen's work hinges on a heightened phenomenal sense engendered by the transformations of projective geometry. As an extension of these concerns, the Specific relies on geometry and perception to articulate the habitation of architecture as well as architecture's external habitation. Geometry and perception become the means to bring the site and the structure into a particular relation.

Regarding the complementary notion of a layered space and time, as discussed above, the specific is contingent on both urban and landscape constructs wherein a structure is created by an accrued use through time. The specific also relies on a set of internal operations that generate overlaid simulations of use through the structure. These notions of layering and accretion define the work of Enric Miralles's. Structural, formal and spatial intents began to accumulate in a represen-

  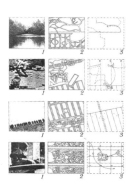

"The gestures determining my work come from a specific set of interests, irrespective of the ensuing spatial results. I believe that systematic repetition and variation can provide coherence and a great deal of my work depends upon repetitive accumulation and repetition. I rework every sketch at least thirty times, and my colleagues do the same. My repetitive method is aimed at revealing the underlying structure of the site, its scale and its basic coordinates. Repetition is essential to the embodiment of an architectural idea. I work with constructive rather than visual criteria, and in this respect repetition assumes a statical significance. Geometry is important as a basic tool, affording a means of articulating specific situations and leading towards forms that could not have been anticipated at the beginning."

Enric Miralles [24]

tational space as a preamble for a saturated tectonic world. The result of which are projects of such density that certain paths—the diagonal was always present in his work—intensify the phenomenal habitation of said structures.

In Tschumi's descriptions of his Manhattan Transcripts, he foregrounds the 'solidification of movement'. A narrative action is played out in space; it is procedurally sequenced and notationally transcribed into vectors and forms. The exceptional conceit is to take a bizarre single occurring action and to transform it into the program for an architecture. Tschumi's operation was widely welcomed for not only proposing a connection to something outside the discipline, but also for incorporating other possible and tangible non-linguistic concerns for architecture's engenderment. Though the implication of solidified movement is implicit in the specific mode, it does not intend to transcribe a single occurring action but rather to induce a set of activities into a legible choreography.

The construction of space in the generic is inherently social and programmatic. It relies on activators (charged particles within a container), on relational logics, and on the permutable coming and goings of the inhabitants within the space. In this sense, it is a *configurative* field. The construction of space in the specific is defined by pattern and function. It establishes a defined pattern within the larger field and in this sense it is *figural*. The term figural refers to several traits: an antonym of ground, a metaphorical reference, and representations of human and animal likeness. Although this

compendium of interpretations may all apply to a *figural* characteristic of a specific space, the last trait seems to add a dimension of layering and determination in the production of space. This is because space in the specific conforms to the layered inscription of the field and to the structure. There is an *adaptive* geometry that is instinctual and opportunistic rather than social. The specific space structures the sensorial and it orchestrates its decision making in conjunction with a series of architectural operations that amplify these relationships in space. These architectural operations can range from projective geometries that incorporate perspectival relationships into the shaping of the structure to demands of use, topography, and other environmental factors. The Lasso House and other works to follow develop a range of *Specific* architectural types whose registers further explain the qualities of the *Specific*.

Left to Right :
Parc dels Colors, Enric Miralles –
Benedetta Tagliabue Arquitectes
Associates, 2002
Manhattan Transcripts, Bernard

Tschumi, 1976-1989
"Rotated Orthographic Projection",
Piero della Francesca, 15th century
Tel Aviv Museum of Art, Preston
Scott Cohen, 2010

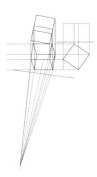
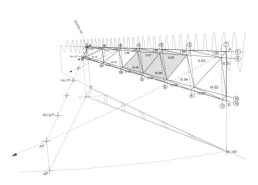

Scalar Architecture
Playing The Specific Generic Field
by Ivan Rupnik

In architectural practice, carefully construed and rigorously consistent disciplinary preoccupations are all too frequently sidelined by the more banal demands of professional practices. As a result young designers attempt to remedy this dichotomy between the desires of the discipline and the pragmatics of the profession through a less than satisfying shortcuts; either maintaining a formal consistency at the cost of the productive contingencies of a specific project or through the deployment of pseudo-intellectual discourse intended to give relevance to an otherwise unrelated body of work. Even the attempt to define a disciplinary position through the wholehearted embrace of the pragmatics of the profession has not guaranteed an integration of these two poles of architectural practice.

Julio Salcedo, the founding partner of Scalar Architects, has developed a working resolution of this schizophrenic condition faced by many young practices. A broader disciplinary preoccupation with the notions of generic and specific in architecture has emerged from two experiments in professional practice, the Lasso House and the SVS House. The disciplinary field drawn between these two houses has informed Scalar's other projects without the need for a reductive formal consistency or an artificially applied theoretical discourse, with each project finding a space in the specific generic field, expanding the architectural potency of this working hypothesis.

The two poles of Salcedo's disciplinary preoccupation share a common program; they are both second homes, functioning as natural retreats for their owners. Their similarities end here. The Lasso House (2001), located on the northern coast of Spain defines the specific end of the spectrum, while the SVS House (2005), located on a lake near the coast of Maine holds the generic side.

Lasso House is carefully calibrated to its context and calibrates it in turn. Instead of an object placed on a landscape it seems to arise from the intersection of existing fault lines articulated through a kind of spatial cross or knot. The house has the smallest possible gesture with the largest possible grasp, a far reaching tight glove. As a specific object it is neither reproducible on a different site nor repeatable on this one. The highly tuned spatial structure is echoed in the material and tectonic qualities of the house.

While the Lasso House's specific relationship to its natural context evokes the tight fit of medieval hill towns, rationally aligned to an irregular geometry, the SVS House borrows from the generic logic of urban planning, relying on the compact deployment of programmed elements into a regular grid for the generation of spatial richness. Aloof from the surrounding context, the observer is presented a series of

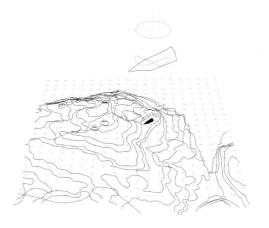

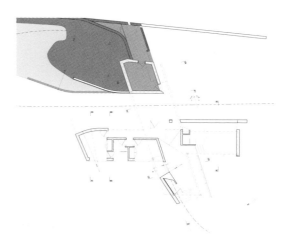

dynamic internal spaces existing between more tightly de-fined volumes set against the loose perimeter. The house's interior structure is infinitely redeployable and the object is itself repeatable. The generic special structure parallels the prefabricated and at least partially ready-made material and tectonic logic of the building.

While defining two opposing poles of the specific generic continuum, Lasso House and the SVS House share a certain design approach which could be called scalar. This approach allows these two projects to exceed their shared typology and function topologically, creating a high density of relation-ships, these relationships in turn generating interconnected spaces of widely varied scales, thereby generating a sca-lar condition. For the Lasso House this topological density is generated through a feedback loop of physical and visual scalar extensions to the landscape it is a translation of. This translational and somewhat distanced relationship prevents this project from reverting to the formal tropes of many sup-posedly topologically driven architectures. The high degree of tension generated the rapidly oscillating jumps in scalar relationships between building and landscape, a highly extro-verted approach, is matched in the SVS House by a similar density of varying relationships, albeit in a highly introverted sense. The division of that project into a tight envelope and a set of loosely placed highly precise volumes generated a

dense field of relationship with no external reference to ele-ments outside of the project, an abstract and highly genera-tive spatial system instead of an abstraction or idealization of an element of reference residing outside of the project; externality, difference, even specificity lie outside of the proj-ect, in the realm of the user's experience.

A satisfying symmetry exists between the shared scalar strategy that allows these two houses to operate beyond their familiar program and humble scale and their role as the fixed poles of a broader disciplinary and professional project, the specific generic continuum, which is the working hypoth-esis of this volume.

IVAN RUPNIK. Architect, urban designer, professor and theorist works be-tween Boston and Zagreb. Rupnik coauthored *Project Zagreb: Transition as Condition, Strategy, Practice*, a book published by Actar and Harvard Uni-versity that explores the types of architectural design practices that emerge in context of prolonged instability. Also at Harvard, Rupnik's PhD work re-searches the notion of experimentation as distinct from avant-garde architec-tural practice in post war theory and practice. Rupnik is assistant Professor at Northeastern University's School of Architecture and he is currently working on a 100 hectare university campus in collaboration with the Spatial Planning Office of the University of Zagreb and an urban park and infrastructural node in collaboration with HPNJ+ Architects, also in Zagreb.

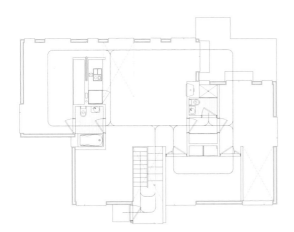

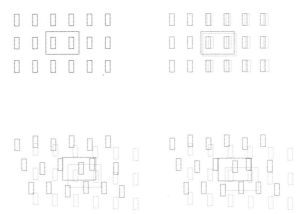

From **Specific** **to** **Generic**
Four projects spanning the Continuum

A Photographic Tour

The four projects spanning the continuum from the *Specific* 'Lasso House', to 'Recess', onto 'Woodstock / Wellfleet' and reaching the *Generic* 'SVS House', are shown in photographs with some explanatory diagrams. The transition pages between the projects highlight the architectural techniques and registers that linked the projects beyond their representation in photographs. These diagrams are windows into the design operations that produced the projects and defined the *Continuum*. The photographs stand as records of the effects of the *Continuum* as well as the exuberance and independence of architectural implementation.

LASSO HOUSE

RECESS

WELLFLEET / WOODSTOCK

SVS HOUSE

LASSO HOUSE

At the specific end of the Continuum, Lasso House's architecture is adaptive, figurative and taut. Lasso House, a 1,700-square-foot residential structure, is located near the small village of Trasierra on Spain's North Atlantic coast. Emerging from a sloping windswept former cornfield overlooking the Gulf of Biscay, Lasso House intertwines the built structure with the landscape. An accretion of desired design traces—acknowledging topography, prevailing winds, rain patterns, views and a perambulation of the site—adaptively generated the form of a figure of eight along the site's longest diagonal and complementary northwestern orientation. The structure is composed around a series of hinges or vertical axes occurring at the moment of crossing within the figure of eight. This technique defies standard projective geometry, which focuses on elevations and façades, in favor of an alternative projective composition that develops about the axis and the spaces in-between. The quadrants of the nexus are programmed as alternatively public or private in alignment with the resultant geometry. Lasso House is a closely draped structure around both a discreet perceptual sequence and environmental conditions.

Its tautness heightens and amplifies the sequence of arrival, passage, linkage and occupation; ultimately, Lasso House's very specificity furthers the interdependence of structure, geometry and the larger realm.

INTRICA-TE-CY   ADAPT-IVE-ED   FIGUR-AL-ATIVE

> SPECIFIC

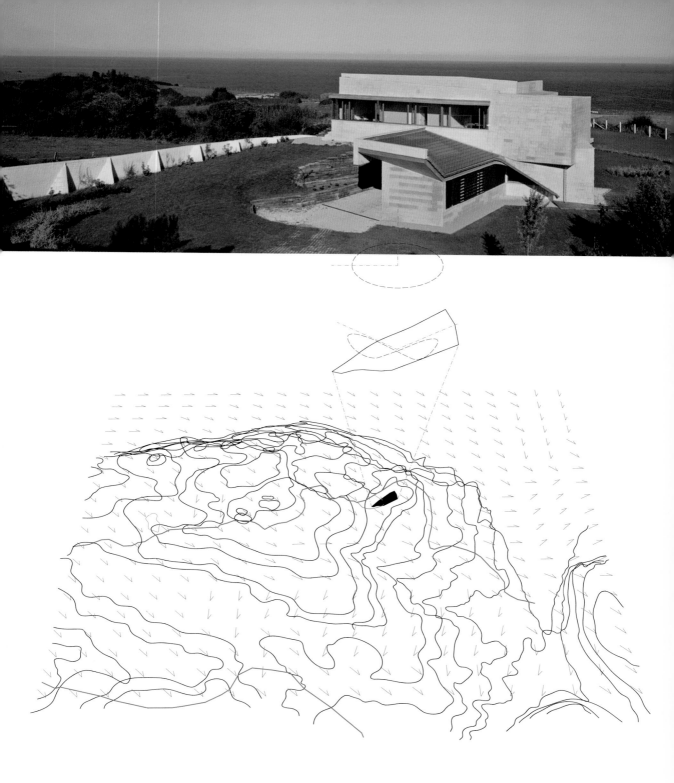

Left Aerial view of site
Above Ocean view and site diagram

Left View of western quadrant
Above Property wall
Following Spread View of southwestern quadrant

Above View of living room
Right Back entrance

Left Stair handrail
Above View of interior stair

Left View of
southwestern quadrant

Left View of eastern quadrant
Above Dusk views
Following Spread View of southeastern quadrant

Right View of dining area

Left View of
northern quadrant

Above Main entry
Left Second floor balcony
Right Salvaged wood wall
Following Spread View of western quadrant

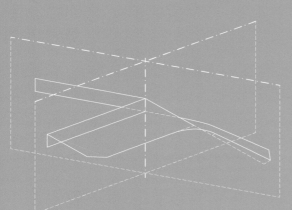

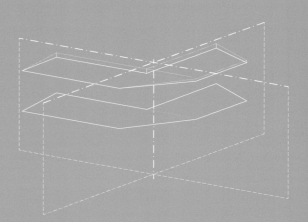

GENERIC <

RECESS

Spanning the *Generic Specific Continuum*, Recess manages to address most of its qualities and registers. This is due to the fact that the design is devised around two complementary halves: the lower exemplifying the *Specific*, and the upper the *Generic*. Fabricated with sustainable materials in New York City, Recess is the first 'prototype' of a new culinary and lifestyle venture. The lower half is a patterned surface of "plyboo"— a rapidly renewable laminated bamboo composite. This surface constructs a figurative, adaptive and intricate landscape of lean-to walls, tables, counters and benches. By enabling customers to both lean and sit on its surfaces, this inner landscape engages the physical habitation of the space by ergonomically adapting to the activities of ordering, lounging and eating. The upper half, built out of fabric and recycled metal, configures a field that serves as a mutable backdrop for different activities. This upper configuration engages the senses through the interplay of light, color, sound and reflection to create different moods that respond to music, the seasons and the time of the day. Recess is the time to diverge from the norm. Drawing from its urban setting, the design establishes a connection to other spaces that offer a laidback milieu—like the neighboring greenspaces— while re-introducing the urban configurative field above as an enabler of moods and activities.

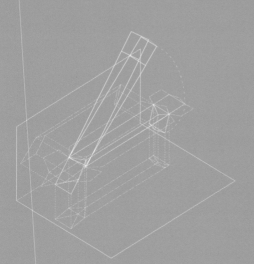

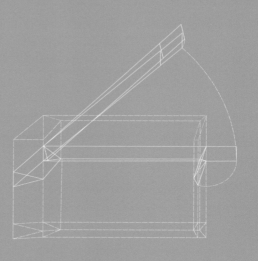

| INTRICA-TE-CY | ADAPT-IVE-ED | FIGUR-AL-ATIVE |

> SPECIFIC

Left Communal table and service counter
Above Site plan and project diagrams

Left Storefront

frozen yogurt

original tart
each topping .65
small $2.95   combo $4.45
medium $3.95   combo $5.45
large $6.95   combo $7.95

pomegranate / featured flavors
small $3.95   combo $5.45
medium $4.95   combo $6.45
large $7.45   combo $8.95

smoothies
small 16 oz $4.95   large 24 oz $5.45
ry berry blackberry, blueberry, strawberry, raspberry, banana
ngo madness mango, pineapple, strawberry, banana
nge oasis orange juice, strawberry, banana
t peachy peach, mango, strawberry, banana
vi strawberry kiwi, strawberry, banana
eapple express pineapple, mango, banana
ke your own whatever you desire
smoothies are blended with juice, ice and frozen yogurt

coffee / espre
small 16 oz   large
house blend $1.95
latte $2.25
vanilla latte $2.75
caramel latte $2.75
cappuccino $2.25
caramel cappuccino $2.75
mocha $2.25
hot cocoa $1.75
mochaccino $2.75
mint mochaccino $2.75
flavors (vanilla, cinnamon, mint, caramel) 50¢

Left Counter and product menu
Above Communal table
Following Spread Configurative ceiling field

Left Dining interior
Above Sidetable
Right Leanwall

OPEN-END-ED-NESS

GENERIC <

WELLFLEET/ WOODSTOCK

Navigating the *Generic Specific Continuum* towards the generic pole, Wellfleet / Woodstock's architecture is *configural* and *figural, taut* and *loose* at different scales. The project originated as a commission for the expansion of the Woodstock Artist Association Museum in Woodstock, New York, and later evolved into a writer's structure in Wellfleet, Massachusetts. Both proposals are *configural* at the scale of their structure and skin while *figural* and *taut* at the scale of the building. The space remains *loose* at all scales. The seriality of structural and skin elements permutates to incorporate the lateral forces upon them. This overt permutation of the structural elements introduces a figuration on their perimeter—a triangular 'gambrel' to address moment connections on its frame. Consequently, the architecture becomes taut where the geometry of the exterior perimeter transforms to maintain a legible prismatic interior space while incorporating the structural mandates. The figurative and taut conditions of the structure create a field with the existing pitched roof structures; whereas the loose quality of the space affords lax transitions from the existing building to proposed structures and to the town and/or landscape beyond.

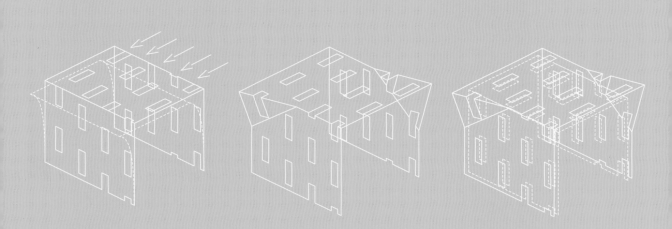

TAUT-NESS   FIGUR-AL-ATIVE

> SPECIFIC

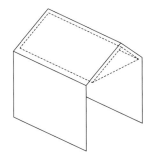

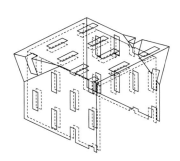

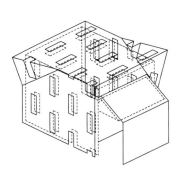
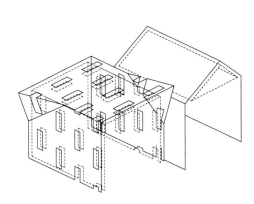

Far Left Computer renderings for Woodstock Artists Association Museum
Left Site and structure frame deformation diagrams for Woodstock and Wellfleet
Above Wellfleet artists retreat and existing structure beyond

Above and Right Pavilion at night

Left Interior view
Above Skylight view

Left View to exterior landscape
Above Front façade

Above and Right Gambrel ends and detail

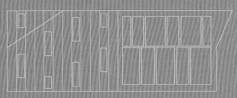

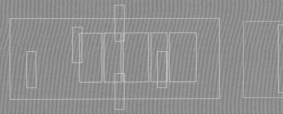

CONFIGUR-AL-ATIVE   LOOSE-NESS   OPEN-END-ED-NESS

GENERIC <

SVS HOUSE

At the *Generic* end of the *Continuum*, the SVS house is *loose, open-ended, complex* and *configural*. The SVS house, a 115 square foot locally sourced structure, is located on a heavily wooded site on the shore of Branch Lake, Maine. The woods are a nuanced field of assorted plant densities varying in slope and luminosity. The program required flexibility and multiple performance possibilities for inhabitants ranging from a single artist to a large family. In time, the house will grow to the unfinished lower level. The design evolved from our research of Peter and Alison Smithson's 1959 unrealized project for a retirement house. The plan's first impression of a quotidian Mies van der Rohe plan—a cultural generic of borrowed typologies and elements—corresponds to our play on the local balloon frame / ranch style construction. A second reading reveals an excess of elements and unexpected relationships—another definition of the *generic* being an emergence of a complex *configurative* system. Likewise, our plan does not rely on figurative compositional techniques but rather draws from the richness of adjacencies, alignments and overlaps to generate its programmatic performance, its spatial intricacy and ultimately, its architectural appearance. The definition of the SVS house and its site relation relied on *configuration*. Matrices of program filled solids and paired voids are parametrically deployed across the site. The cohabitation of these two matrices affords a complex reading of space both as a discreet set of elements and a loose, open-ended landscape. The relation of the architecture to the larger realm is then doubly confronted by both an internal *Generic* field and its overlaid condition on the aforementioned nuanced field of the woods.

> SPECIFIC

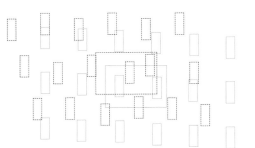

Above and Far Right View to house from the shore
Right Concept and site diagrams

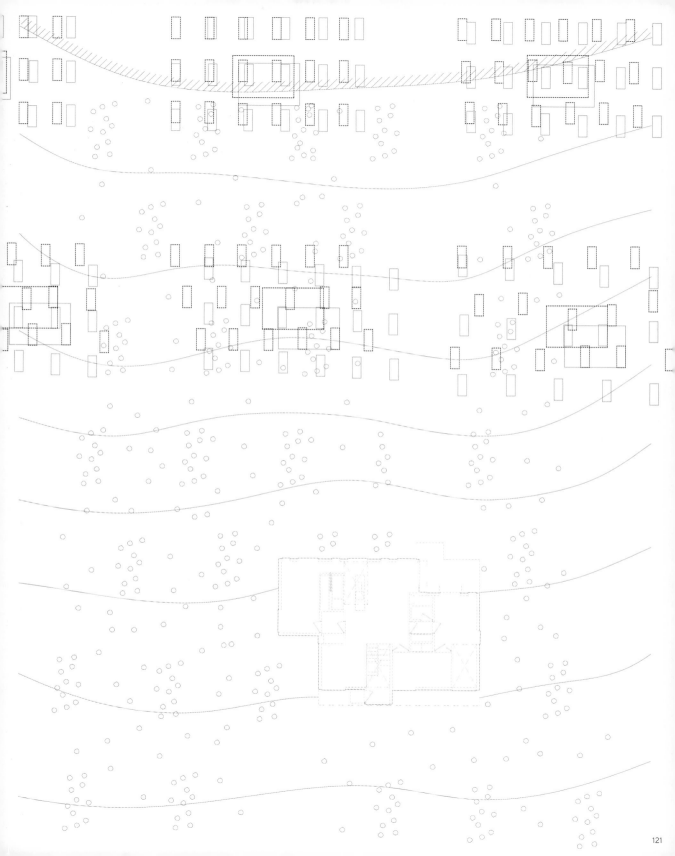

Left View of the front from
the driveway

Below Plans and diagrams of Peter and Alison
Smithson's 1959 project and the SVS House
Left and Right Entry and corner details
Following Spread Front elevation

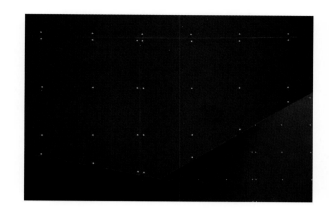

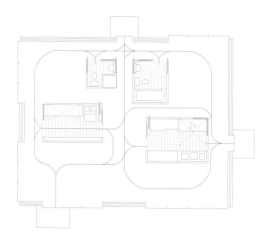

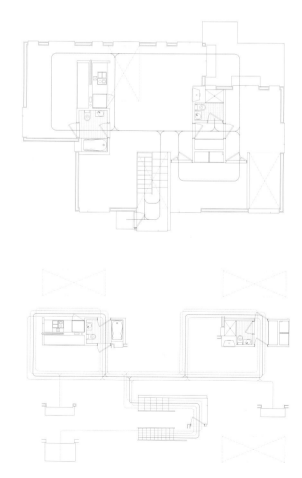

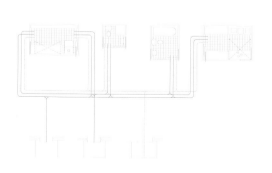

Right View of drawing room, dining room
and front entrance
Following Spread Construction process

Right View from entrance
Above Living room skylight detail

Left Front façade

Left The house at sunset
Above Back façade at night

Above Rear balcony and construction detail
Right Construction detail

Above View to the woods
Right Rear balcony
Following Spread Rear view

From Generic to Specific
Four projects spanning the Continuum

A Projective tour

The four projects spanning the *Continuum*—from the *Generic* 'SVS House', through 'Woodstock / Wellfleet', onto 'Recess' and reaching the *Specific* 'Lasso House'—are represented with their projective documents. On their own, these projections neither suffice to bring forth the richness of the projects in terms of their organization and perceptual program—to name only two parameters—nor can they be explained without a larger understanding of the *Continuum*. These projections are two-dimensional frames of the final moments in the gestation of these projects. The plans, sections and elevations stand as tools of future implementations and as a record of current actions and configurations. They are the repository space of the intricacies of projection as it sets out to produce the richness of the *Continuum.*

SVS HOUSE

WELLFLEET / WOODSTOCK

RECESS

LASSO HOUSE

SVS HOUSE

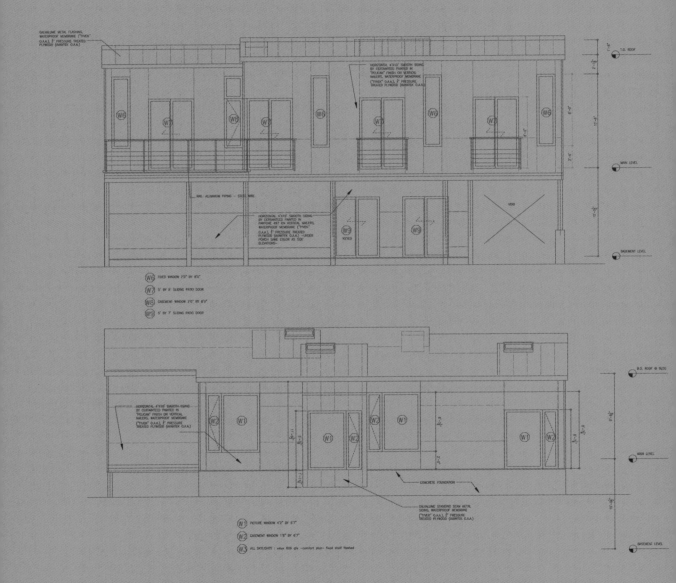

Elevations

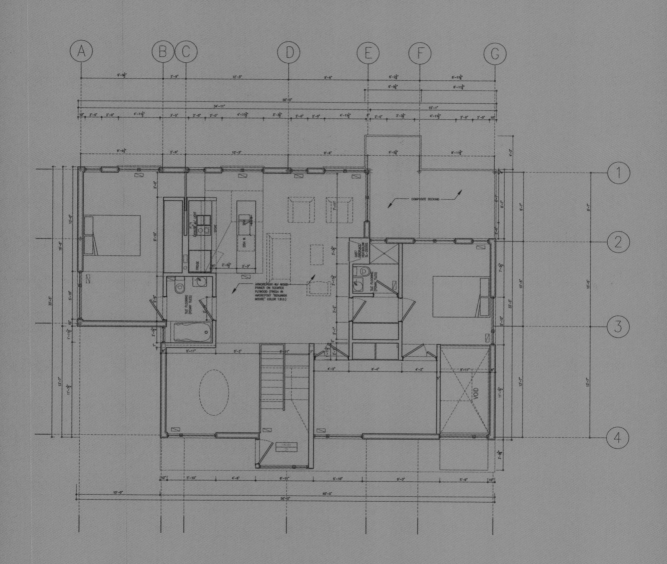

Ground Floor Plan

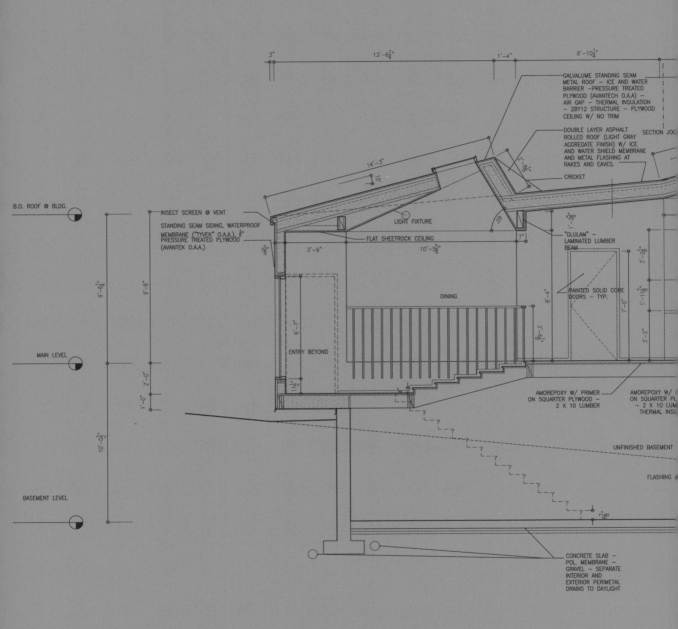

GALVALUME STANDING SEAM
METAL ROOF – ICE AND WATER
BARRIER –PRESSURE TREATED
PLYWOOD (AVANTECH O.A.A) –
AIR GAP – THERMAL INSULATION
– 2BY12 STRUCTURE – PLYWOOD
CEILING W/ NO TRIM

DOUBLE LAYER ASPHALT
ROLLED ROOF (LIGHT GRAY
AGGREGATE FINISH) W/ ICE
AND WATER SHIELD MEMBRANE
AND METAL FLASHING AT
RAKES AND EAVES.

SECTION JOG

CRICKET

"GLULAM" –
LAMINATED LUMBER
BEAM

PAINTED SOLID CORE
DOORS – TYP.

B.O. ROOF @ BLDG.

INSECT SCREEN @ VENT

STANDING SEAM SIDING, WATERPROOF
MEMBRANE ("TYVEK" O.A.A.),
PRESSURE TREATED PLYWOOD
(AVANTEK O.A.A.)

LIGHT FIXTURE

FLAT SHEETROCK CEILING

DINING

ENTRY BEYOND

MAIN LEVEL

AMOREPOXY W/ PRIMER
ON 5QUARTER PLYWOOD –
2 X 10 LUMBER

AMOREPOXY W/
ON 5QUARTER PL
– 2 X 10 LUM
THERMAL INSU

UNFINISHED BASEMENT

FLASHING

BASEMENT LEVEL

CONCRETE SLAB –
POL. MEMBRANE –
GRAVEL – SEPARATE
INTERIOR AND
EXTERIOR PERIMETAL
DRAINS TO DAYLIGHT

Cross Section

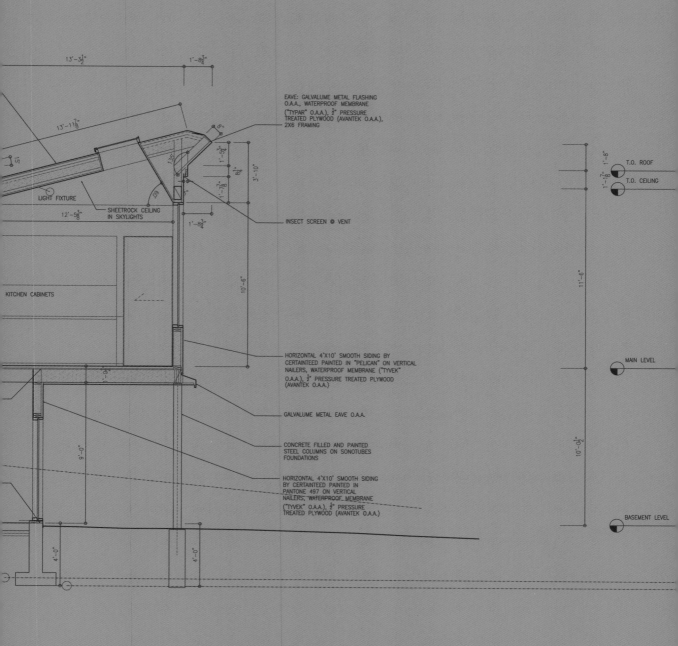

13'-3½"

1'-8¾"

13'-11⅞"

EAVE: GALVALUME METAL FLASHING
O.A.A., WATERPROOF MEMBRANE
("TYPAR" O.A.A.), ½" PRESSURE
TREATED PLYWOOD (AVANTEK O.A.A.),
2X6 FRAMING

15°

3'-10"

LIGHT FIXTURE

SHEETROCK CEILING
IN SKYLIGHTS

12'-5⅜"

1'-8½"

INSECT SCREEN @ VENT

10'-6"

KITCHEN CABINETS

HORIZONTAL 4'X10' SMOOTH SIDING BY
CERTAINTEED PAINTED IN "PELICAN" ON VERTICAL
NAILERS, WATERPROOF MEMBRANE ("TYVEK"
O.A.A.), ½" PRESSURE TREATED PLYWOOD
(AVANTEK O.A.A.)

GALVALUME METAL EAVE O.A.A.

CONCRETE FILLED AND PAINTED
STEEL COLUMNS ON SONOTUBES
FOUNDATIONS

9'-0"

HORIZONTAL 4'X10' SMOOTH SIDING
BY CERTAINTEED PAINTED IN
PANTONE 497 ON VERTICAL
NAILERS, WATERPROOF MEMBRANE
("TYVEK" O.A.A.), ½" PRESSURE
TREATED PLYWOOD (AVANTEK O.A.A.)

4'-0"

4'-0"

1'-8"

T.O. ROOF

1'-1⅞"

T.O. CEILING

11'-6"

MAIN LEVEL

10'-0½"

BASEMENT LEVEL

149

WELLFLEET / WOODSTOCK

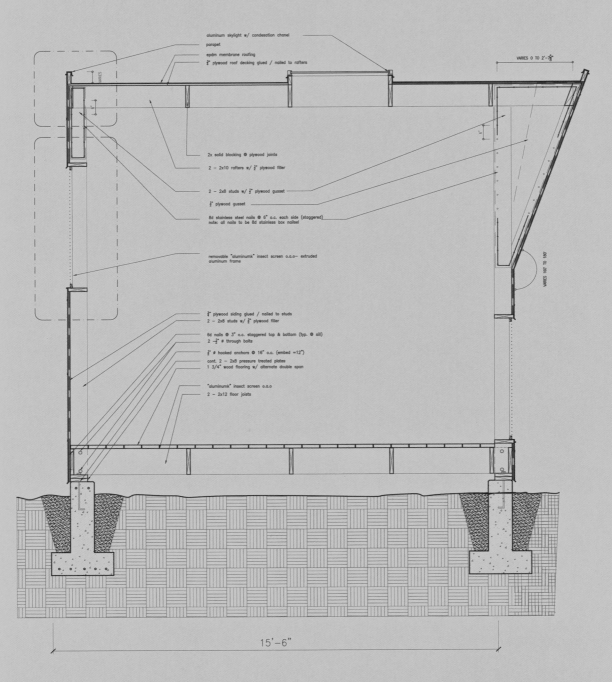

aluminum skylight w/ condesation chanel

parapet

epdm membrane roofing

$\frac{3}{4}$" plywood roof decking glued / nailed to rafters

VARIES 0 TO 2'-7$\frac{5}{8}$"

2x solid blocking @ plywood joints

2 – 2x10 rafters w/ $\frac{1}{2}$" plywood filler

2 – 2x8 studs w/ $\frac{1}{2}$" plywood gusset

$\frac{1}{2}$" plywood gusset

8d stainless steel nails @ 6" o.c. each side (staggered)
note: all nails to be 8d stainless box nails!

removable "aluminumk" insect screen o.a.o– extruded
aluminum frame

VARIES 16/7 TO 18/7

$\frac{3}{4}$" plywood siding glued / nailed to studs

2 – 2x8 studs w/ $\frac{1}{2}$" plywood filler

6d nails @ 3" o.c. staggered top & bottom (typ. @ sill)

2 –$\frac{1}{2}$" ϕ through bolts

$\frac{3}{4}$" ϕ hooked anchors @ 16" o.c. (embed =12")

cont. 2 – 2x8 pressure treated plates

1 3/4" wood flooring w/ alternate double span

"aluminumk" insect screen o.a.o

2 – 2x12 floor joists

15'-6"

Cross Section

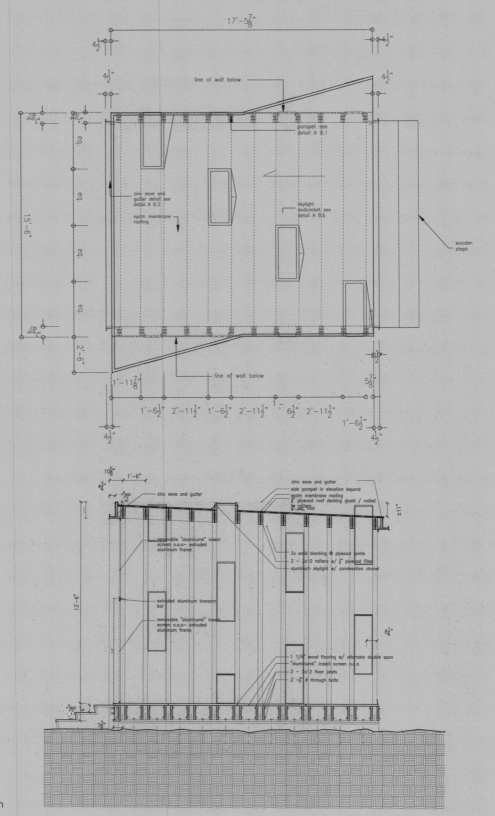

line of wall below

parapet see
detail A 8.1

zinc eave and
gutter detail see
detail A 8.3

epdm membrane
roofing

skylight
andcricket, see
detail A 8,6

wooden
steps

17'-5⅞"

15'-6"

eq.

eq.

eq.

eq.

line of wall below

4½"

4½"

4½"

4½"

4½"

4½"

8¾"

8¾"

2'-6"

1'-11⅞"

5⅞"

1'-6½"   2'-11½"   1'-6½"   2'-11½"   6½"   2'-11½"

1'-6½"

zinc eave and gutter

side parapet in elevation beyond
epdm membrane roofing
plywood roof decking glued / nailed

10⅝"   1'-6"

zinc eave and gutter

removable "aluminumk" insect
screen o.a.o- extruded
aluminum frame

2x solid blocking @ plywood joints
2 - 2x10 rafters w/ ½" plywood filler
aluminum skylight w/ condesation chanel

extruded aluminum transom
bar

removable "aluminumk" insect
screen o.a.o- extruded
aluminum frame

13'-6"

8¼"

1 1/4" wood flooring w/ alternate double span
"aluminumk" insect screen o.a.o
2 - 2x12 floor joists
2 - ¾" Ø through bolts

±11"

Roof Plan Section

RECESS

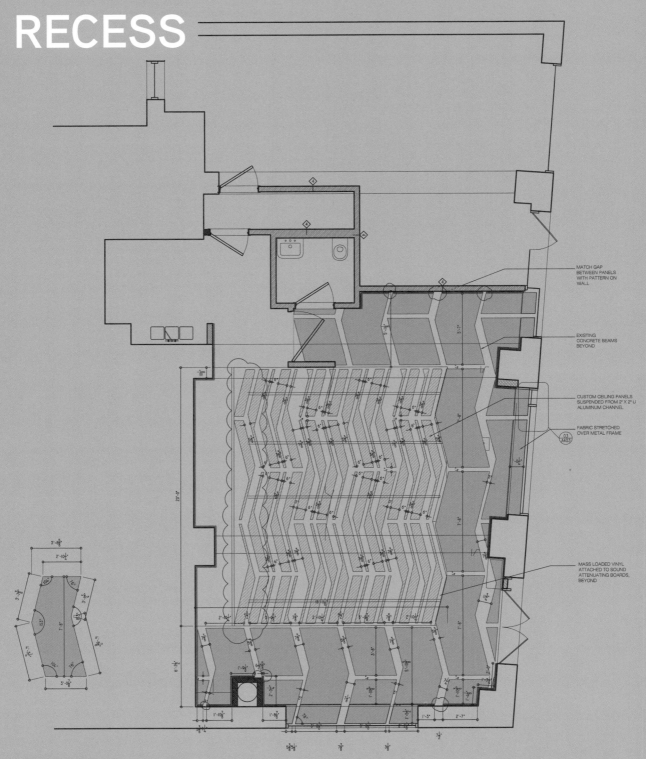

MATCH GAP
BETWEEN PANELS
WITH PATTERN ON
WALL

EXISTING
CONCRETE BEAMS
BEYOND

CUSTOM CEILING PANELS
SUSPENDED FROM 2" X 2" U
ALUMINUM CHANNEL

FABRIC STRETCHED
OVER METAL FRAME

MASS LOADED VINYL
ATTACHED TO SOUND
ATTENUATING BOARDS,
BEYOND

Reflected Ceiling Plan

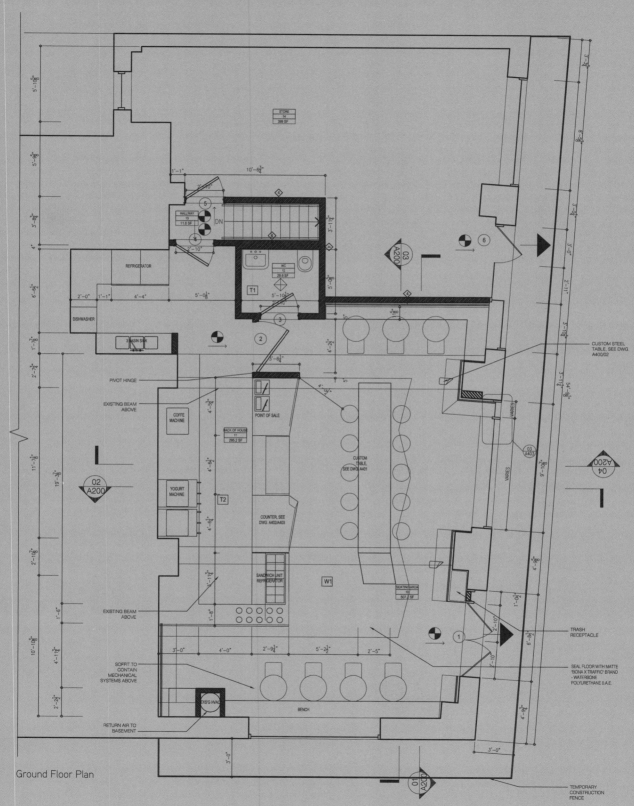

Ground Floor Plan

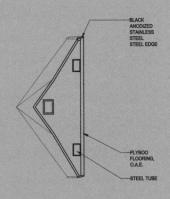

BLACK
ANODIZED
STAINLESS
STEEL
STEEL EDGE

PLYBOO
FLOORING,
O.A.E.

STEEL TUBE

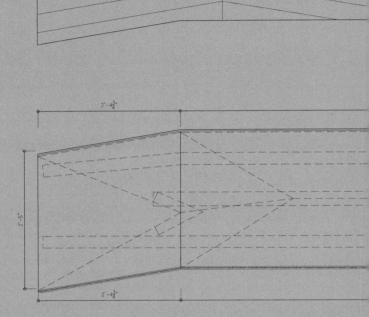

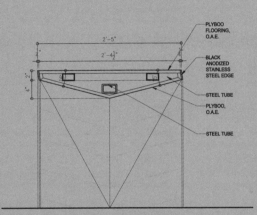

PLYBOO
FLOORING,
O.A.E.

BLACK
ANODIZED
STAINLESS
STEEL EDGE

STEEL TUBE

PLYBOO,
O.A.E.

STEEL TUBE

2'-5"

2'-4½"

2'-4¾"

2'-5"

2'-4¾"

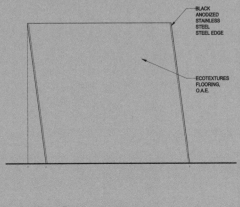

BLACK
ANODIZED
STAINLESS
STEEL
STEEL EDGE

ECOTEXTURES
FLOORING,
O.A.E.

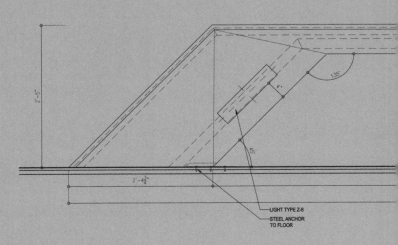

2'-5"

135°

4"

45°

2'-4¾"

LIGHT TYPE Z-6

STEEL ANCHOR
TO FLOOR

Custom Table Details

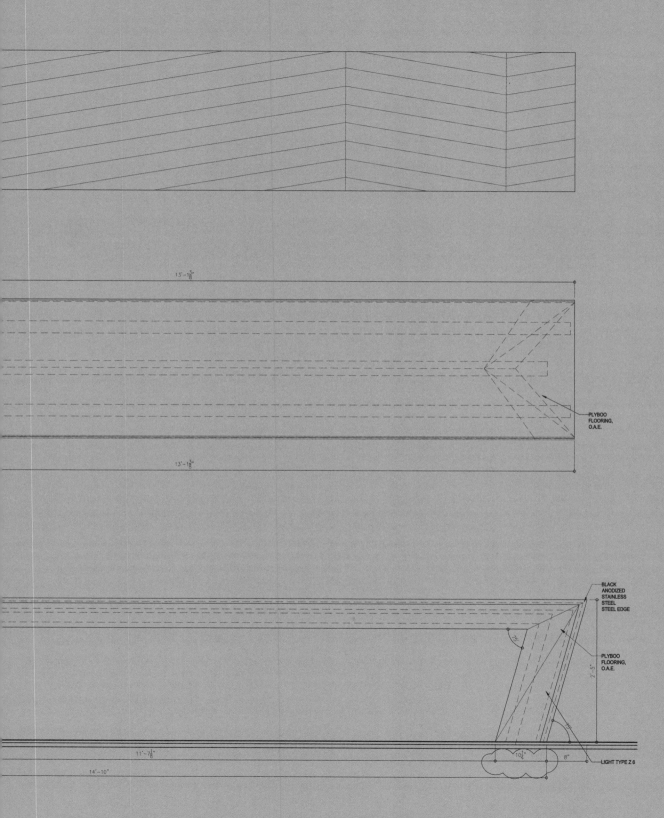

13'−1⅞"

13'−1⅞"

PLYBOO
FLOORING,
O.A.E.

BLACK
ANODIZED
STAINLESS
STEEL
STEEL EDGE

75°

2'−5"

PLYBOO
FLOORING,
O.A.E.

11'−7⅞"

10¼"

8"

LIGHT TYPE Z 6

14'−10"

LASSO
HOUSE

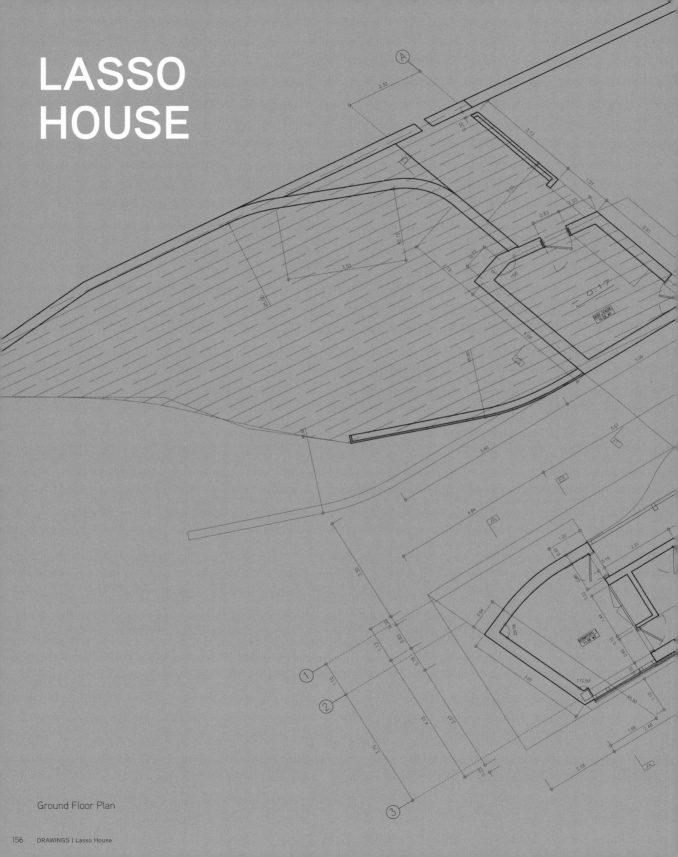

Ground Floor Plan

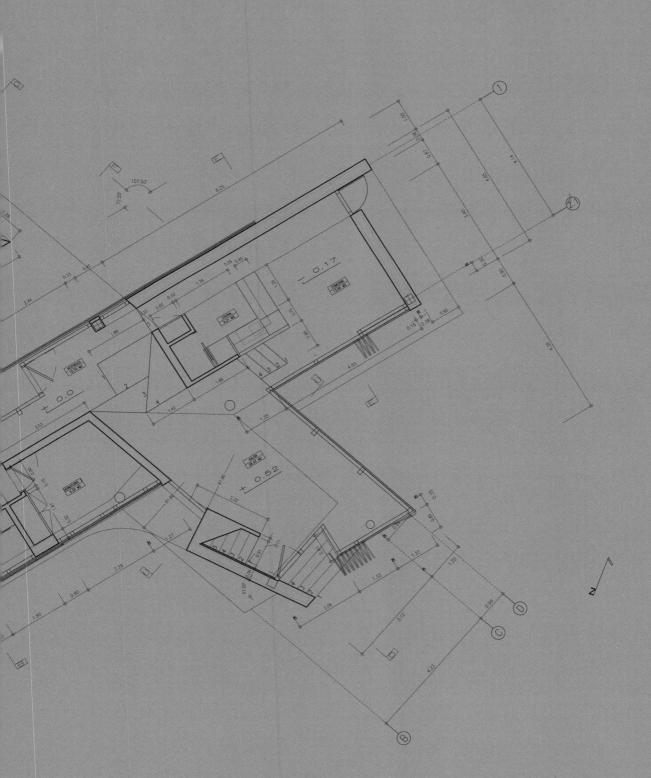

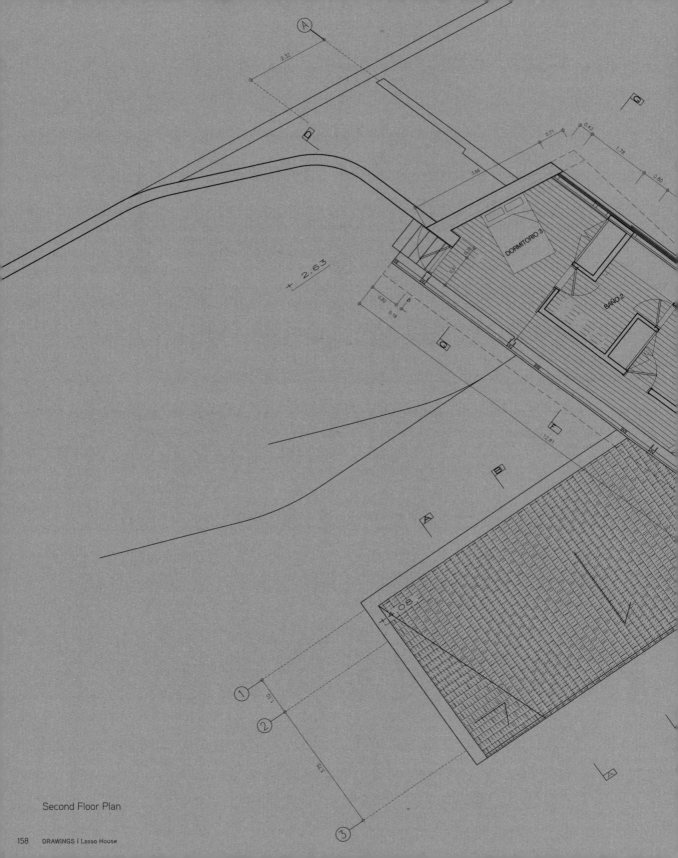

Second Floor Plan

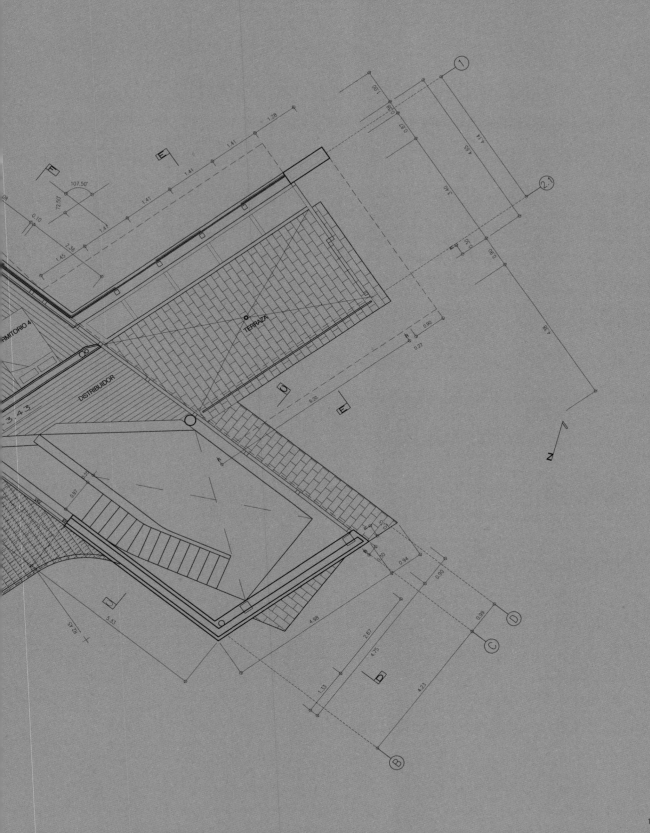

TERRAZA

DISTRIBUIDOR

DORMITORIO 4

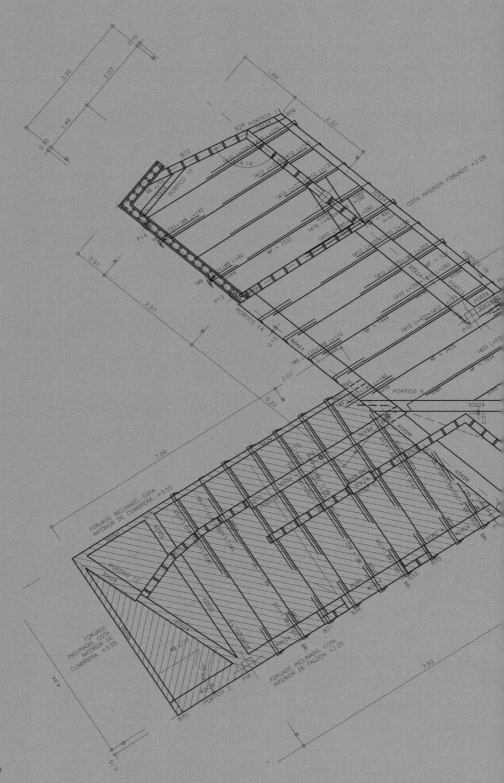

Basement Floor Structural Plan

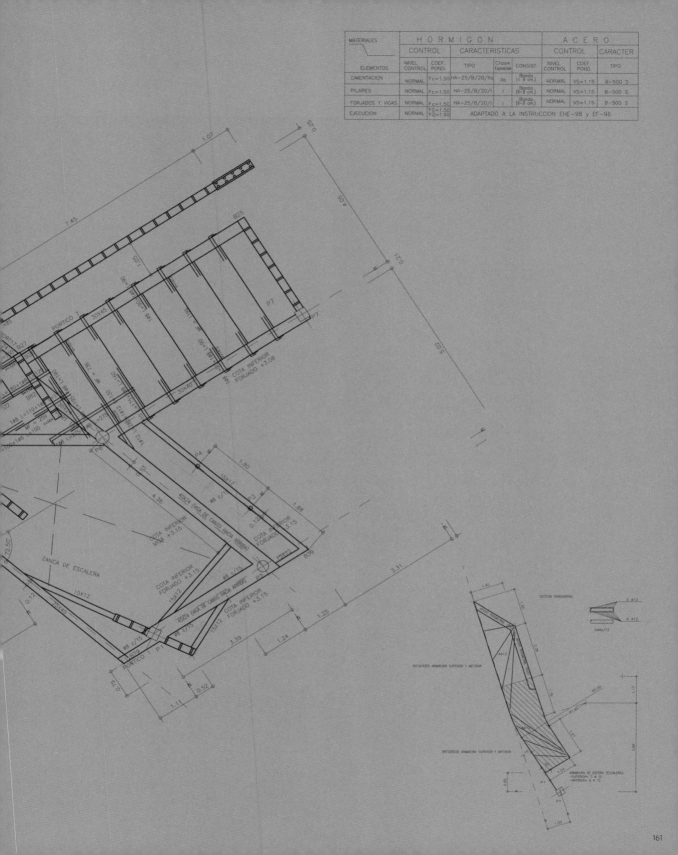

MATERIALES		HORMIGON					ACERO		
		CONTROL		CARACTERISTICAS			CONTROL		CARACTER
ELEMENTOS		NIVEL CONTROL	COEF. POND.	TIPO	Clase Exposicion	CONSIST.	NIVEL CONTROL	COEF. POND.	TIPO
CIMENTACION		NORMAL	$\gamma c=1.50$	HA-25/B/20/IIa	IIa	Blanda (< 9 cm.)	NORMAL	VS=1.15	B-500 S
PILARES		NORMAL	$\gamma c=1.50$	HA-25/B/20/I	I	Blanda (8-9 cm.)	NORMAL	VS=1.15	B-500 S
FORJADOS Y VIGAS		NORMAL	$\gamma c=1.50$	HA-25/B/20/I	I	Blanda (8-9 cm.)	NORMAL	VS=1.15	B-500 S
EJECUCION		NORMAL	$\gamma c=1.50$ $\gamma Q=1.60$	ADAPTADO A LA INSTRUCCION EHE-98 y EF-96					

ZANCA DE ESCALERA

COTA INFERIOR FORJADO +3.08

COTA INFERIOR FORJADO +3.15

161

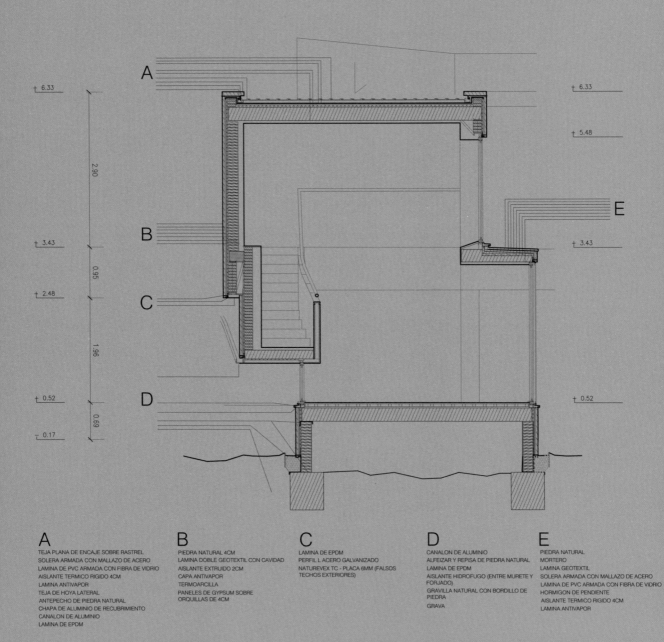

A 6.33

2.90

B 3.43

0.95

2.48

C

1.96

0.52

D

0.69

0.17

6.33

5.48

E

3.43

0.52

A

TEJA PLANA DE ENCAJE SOBRE RASTREL
SOLERA ARMADA CON MALLAZO DE ACERO
LAMINA DE PVC ARMADA CON FIBRA DE VIDRIO
AISLANTE TERMICO RIGIDO 4CM
LAMINA ANTIVAPOR
TEJA DE HOYA LATERAL
ANTEPECHO DE PIEDRA NATURAL
CHAPA DE ALUMINIO DE RECUBRIMIENTO
CANALON DE ALUMINIO
LAMINA DE EPDM

B

PIEDRA NATURAL 4CM
LAMINA DOBLE GEOTEXTIL CON CAVIDAD
AISLANTE EXTRUIDO 2CM
CAPA ANTIVAPOR
TERMOARCILLA
PANELES DE GYPSUM SOBRE
ORQUILLAS DE 4CM

C

LAMINA DE EPDM
PERFIL L ACERO GALVANIZADO
NATUREVEX TC - PLACA 6MM (FALSOS
TECHOS EXTERIORES)

D

CANALON DE ALUMINIO
ALFEIZAR Y REPISA DE PIEDRA NATURAL
LAMINA DE EPDM
AISLANTE HIDROFUGO (ENTRE MURETE Y
FORJADO)
GRAVILLA NATURAL CON BORDILLO DE
PIEDRA
GRAVA

E

PIEDRA NATURAL
MORTERO
LAMINA GEOTEXTIL
SOLERA ARMADA CON MALLAZO DE ACERO
LAMINA DE PVC ARMADA CON FIBRA DE VIDRIO
HORMIGON DE PENDIENTE
AISLANTE TERMICO RIGIDO 4CM
LAMINA ANTIVAPOR

Cross Section

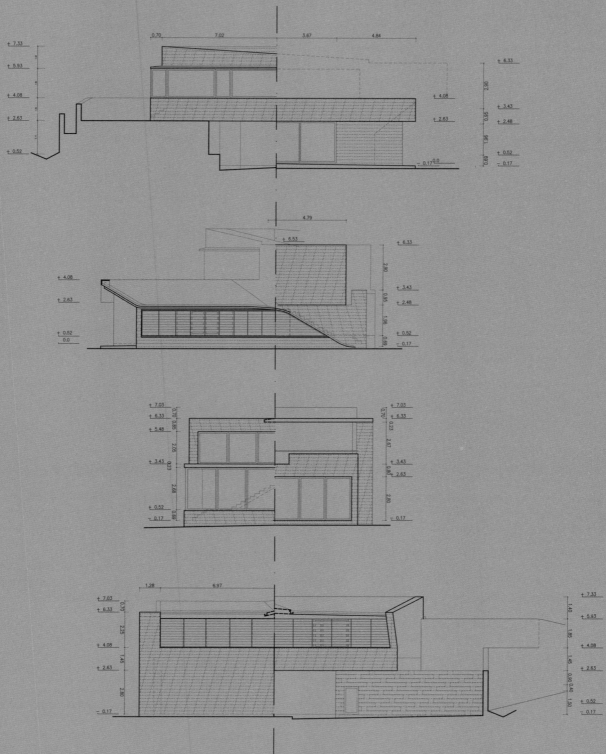

Unhinged Elevations

Endnotes

[1] Lawson, Bryan. Ludwig Wittgenstein quote. *The Language of Space* (Oxford, UK : Architectural Press, 2001) 128.

[2] Lawson, Bryan. Aldo Van Eyck quote. *The Language of Space* (Oxford, UK : Architectural Press, 2001) 128.

[3] Tschumi, Bernard. Guest Lecture. Contextualizing Materials. City College of New York. New York, NY. 15 Oct 2009.

[4] Kostof, Spiro. (1989). The Design of Cities [The Mayors Institute on City Design]. Places, 5(4).
     Retrieved from: http://www.escholarship.org/uc/item/5d25k7jd

[5] Constant, Caroline. "Barcelona Pavilion as Landscape Garden". AA Files: 20. (Fall 1990) pp. 46.

[6] Mayne, Thom. Guest Lecture. Continuity of Contradictions. City College of New York. New York, NY. 5 Nov 2009.

[7] Eric Mumford, Eric. "The Emergence of Mat or Field Buildings." *Case: Le Corbusier's Venice Hospital and the Mat Building Revival*. Eds. Hashim Sarkis, Pablo Allard, and Timothy Hyde (Prestel Publishing: New York, NY 2001) 64.

[8] Sarkis, Hashim. *Case: Le Corbusier's Venice Hospital and the Mat Building Revival*. Eds. Hashim Sarkis, Pablo Allard, and Timothy Hyde (Prestel Publishing: New York, NY 2001) 13.

[9] Marshall, Richard. "Asian Megacities." *Shaping the City*. Ed. Rodolphe El-Khoury and Edward Robins (Routledge: New York, NY 2004) 206.

[10] Evans, Robin. *The Projective Cast*. (MIT Press: Boston, MA 1995) 363.

[11] Balmond, Cecil. *Informal*. (Prestel Publishing: New York, NY 2002) 371.

[12] Reiser, Jesse and Umemoto, Nanako. *Atlas of Novel Tectonics*. (Princeton Architectural Press: New York, NY 2006) 46.

[13] Allen, Stan. Practice: *Architecture, Technique and Representation (Critical Voices in Art, Theory and Culture)*. Eds. Stan Allen and Diana Agrest (Routledge: New York, NY 1999) 108.

[14] Jung, Wolfgang. " Tilting Volutes, Bending Cornices, and Perplexing Angles and Planes." *Conventions of Architectural Drawing: Representation and Misrepresentation*. Eds. James J. Ackerman and Wolfgang Jung (Harvard University Press: Boston, MA, 2001) 101.

[15] Foucault, Michel. "Tying Down Loose Space." *Loose Space*. Ed. Karen A. Franck and Quentin Stevens (Routledge: New York, NY 2006) 26.

[16] Lynn, Greg. *Intricacy*. ICA: Philadelphia, PA 2003.

[17] Goldhagen, Sarah Williams. *"Freedoms Domiciles." Anxious Modernisms, Expirementation in Postwar Architectural Culture. Ed.* Sarah Williams Goldhagen. The MIT Press: Boston, MA.

[18] Koolhaas, Rem. *S, M, L, XL*. Monacelli Press: New York, NY 1997.

[19] FOA. *Crib Sheets: Notes on Contemporary Architectural Architectural Conversation*. Ed. Sylvia Lavin, Helene Furjan, and Penelope Dean (Monacelli Press: New York, NY 1997) 109.

[20] Lynn, Greg. *Crib Sheets: Notes on Contemporary Architectural Architectural Conversation*. Ed. Sylvia Lavin, Helene Furjan, and Penelope Dean (Monacelli Press: New York, NY 1997) 109.

[21] Lootsma, Bart. "Towards a Reflective Architecture". *El Croquis*, Madrid. Issue 84, 2003.

[22] Goldhagen, Sarah Williams. *"Freedoms Domiciles." Anxious Modernisms, Expirementation in Postwar Architectural Culture.* Ed. Sarah Williams Goldhagen. The MIT Press: Boston, MA.

[23] Koolhaas, Rem. *S, M, L, XL*. Monacelli Press: New York, NY 1997.

[24] Miralles, Enric. Guest Lecture. Technology, Place & Architecture. Jerusalem Conference. Jerusalem, Israel. 1996.

Julio Salcedo
and Scalar Architecture

Julio Salcedo, born in Madrid, Spain, studied architecture and sculpture as an undergraduate at Rice University; he completed his architecture studies at Harvard's Graduate School of Design, where he studied under Rafael Moneo and Enric Miralles, among others. Salcedo is an Associate Professor at City College, New York, and has taught courses on design, history and theory of architecture at the Harvard Graduate School of Design, Syracuse University, University of Pennsylvania and Cornell University. Salcedo has also contributed to various periodical including Pasajes, Spain; Praxis, USA; and Arquitectura, Spain.

He is the principal of scalar Architecture, an award winning international design firm based in New York City. scalar Architecture, as the term indicates, operates at a variety of scales collaborating with key expertise at each juncture of architecture and correlated fields. To these collaborations, 'scalar' provides an expansive utilization of architecture and its registers of program, geometry, context, aesthetics and form. The fruits of this work are urban, landscape, institutional, commercial, and residential projects.

scalar's urban collaborative projects comprise of the ongoing first price for the re-development of Hamar, Norway, and chosen entries for Build a Better Burb and Elemental Chile -a low income housing modular competition. Landscape collaborative projects include the design for a large cross-programmed sustainable park in Madrid, Spain. Commercial projects include two sets of US restaurants, Recess and Flurt. Institutional projects include commissioned designs for the Woodstock Association Museum, the offices of the Dean at Cornell School's of Architecture and an ongoing 100,000 sf medical building in NYC. Lastly, scalar's residential work is comprised of dwellings and housing in Spain, Maine, and New York.

A 2006 Young Architect award recipient from the Architectural League, scalar Architecture, has been widely published in the US - Architectural Record, The Architect's Newspaper, Interior Design, Princeton Architectural Press, Breathe, House Beautiful - and abroad in the following countries Canada, Germany, Norway, Belgium, Holland, Spain, Thailand, Japan, and China.

Credits

Author
Julio Salcedo

Essays Contributed By
Luis Rojo
Ivan Rupnik

Book Contributors
Thomas Dalmas
Erica Ko – Editing
Ana Koleva
Eugene Kuo – Graphic design
Elizabeth MacWillie
James Silvestro

Scalar Architecture
Mubeen Ahmad
Sebastian Andia
Chienchuan Chen
Michael Chen
Malachi Connolly
Thomas Dalmas
Mauricio Estelleras
Francesco Gennarini
Jane Kim
Ana Koleva
Johannes Lott
Elizabeth MacWillie (Associate)
Catriona O'connor
Gema Peiro
Shengyi Pu
Jeremy Reed
Bridget Rynne
Marshall Schuster
Monica Torres

Collaborators
Marc Brossa (So Young Park, Joe Mauer,
Guri Nadler, Christine Graziano, Jade Do)
David Fletcher Studio
Syracuse Heart (Kelly Bennett, Colin Simmer,
Joshua Simoneau, Emillio Stokes, Jennifer Tarsio,
Professor Anne Munly)

Image Credits
Scalar Architecture images
Unless otherwise noted, all projects can be credited to the following:
Lasso House: Miguel de Guzman
Recess: Kris Tamburello
Maine: Fabian Birgfield
Wellfleet: Jon Ball/Katie Mota

Introduction Images
Silodam, Amsterdam, Netherlands, 1995-2003.
MVRDV, All Images Property of MVRDV
Expo 2000 NL Pavilion, Hannover, Germany, 1997-2000. MVRDV,
All Images Property of MVRDV
University of Cincinnati Campus Recreation Center, Cincinnati, Ohio,
United States, 1999-2005. Morphosis Architects: All Images Property
of Morphosis Architects
Yokohama, Yokohama, Japan, 1992. Office of Metropolitan Architecture:
All images property of Office of Metropolitan Architecture
Downsview Park, Toronto, Canada, 2000. Office of Metropolitan
Architecture: All images property of Office of Metropolitan Architecture
Les Halles, Paris, France, 2003. Office of Metropolitan Architecture:
All images property of Office of Metropolitan Architecture
Parc de la Villette, Paris, France, 1982-1998. Bernard Tschumi Architects:
All Images Property of Bernard Tschumi Architects.
Manhattan Transcripts, 1976-1989. Bernard Tschumi Architects:
All Images Property of Bernard Tschumi Architects.
Parc del Colors, Mollet de Valles, Barcelona, Spain, 2002. Enric Miralles
– Benedetta Tagliabue Arquitectes Associates: All images property of
Enric Miralles – Benedetta Tagliabue Arquitectes Associates
Tel Aviv Museum of Art, Tel Aviv, Israel, 2010. Preston Scott Cohen, Inc:
All Images Property of Preston Scott Cohen, Inc.

I Would Like to Thank:
Ivan Rupnik for his extensive contributions to our work;
Luis Rojo, Sandro Marpillero and Linda Pollack for their
friendship and scholarship; Dean George Ranalli and City
College for their academic and financial support; Ben
Gilmartin for his demanding editing; everyone at Scalar
for their dedication to our practice; Dean Mark Robbins for
starting this project at Syracuse in 2005; my colleagues
for continuing to make architecture an engaging
environment, and most of all to my family.

Book Credits
Creative Direction by Leo Malinow
Copy Editing by Kit Maude
Original Editing and Design by Scalar Architecture

Oscar Riera Ojeda Publishers

USA

143 South Second Street, Suite 208
Philadelphia, PA 19106-3073
Telephone: 1-215-238-1333

China

Park A, Fangda Cheng
Longjing Belhuan Road, Nanshan
District, Shanzhen 518055, China
Telephone: 755 8336 6138

Argentina

Conde 2847 D
C1428DBM. Buenos Aires
Telephone: 54-11-4543-6289

www.oscarrieraojeda.com
info@oscarrieraojeda.com

Copyright © 2011 by Oscar Riera Ojeda Publishers
ISBN 978-84-9936-1925